Welcome again!

I'm delighted at the success of the first volume of the 'PopMaster Quiz Book' and the feedback about how much you enjoyed the questions (and the answers). I thank every one of you who bought it, making it possible to bring out Volume 2 which, to my mind, is even better, more fun and more challenging than the first outing.

PopMaster goes from strength to strength. In 2014, I presented a live version of the quiz in Manchester – for the second year running – to raise money for the BBC charity Children in Need. Once again it was packed to capacity at a venue almost double the size of the previous year's event; and in October 2015 we were raising money in Cardiff.

At the beginning of 2015, a special live show was staged at Newport's famous Celtic Manor in Wales, to entertain the workforce of Best Western Hotels at their annual conference, and in 2016 we are planning to take the quiz on tour around hotels and other venues, and offer some great prizes to the winning tables. So please keep your eyes peeled for further information about these events – I hope to see some of you in person.

For those who can't make it to these live events, we are also planning a PopMaster nationwide pub quiz at a local near you. Regrettably, I will not be able to join you all at these events!

Question-setters Phil Swern and Neil Myners have once again filled this edition of the book with a great balance of easy, medium and really difficult questions, which I hope you are going to enjoy attempting to answer. And if you do well, then perhaps you'll apply to be a contestant one morning on my Radio 2 show. Enjoy!

Ken Bruce
BBC Radio 2

D0581346

QUIZ 001 POPMASTER

IMPORTANT

The answers to all questions are cunningly printed on the outside column of the page directly after the quiz page you're looking at. The answers are therefore always two pages after the quiz – so the answers to this quiz are on page 6. (Stop! Don't turn and look until you've done the quiz – they are there, we promise you!)

QUESTION 1
Who sang about 'Nutbush City Limits' in 1973?

QUESTION 2
The Darkness reached the Top 10 in 2003 with the song 'I Believe in...' what?

QUESTION 3
Who reached the Top 10 in 1992 with his cover version of 'The Days of Pearly Spencer'?

QUESTION 4
Dusty Springfield's only number one single was a 1966 song called 'You Don't...' what?

QUESTION 5
What three-word song title has provided different hits for Dead or Alive in 1985, Genesis in 1986 and Belinda Carlisle in 1996?

QUESTION 6
Which Welsh band's Top 10 singles in the Noughties included 'Madame Helga', 'Maybe Tomorrow' and 'Moviestar'?

QUESTION 7
The Australian group Icehouse had its biggest UK hit in 1983. What was it called?

QUESTION 8
The songs 'Action', 'The Lies in Your Eyes' and 'The Six Teens' were all hits in the mid-Seventies for which group?

QUESTION 9
Natalie Cole had her only two Top 10 singles in the late Eighties – name either of these songs.

QUESTION 10
Which of Terry Hall's groups had a hit in 1985 with the song 'Thinking of You'?

POPMASTER QUIZ 002

IMPORTANT

The answers to all questions are cunningly printed on the outside column of the page directly after the quiz page you're looking at. The answers are therefore always two pages after the quiz – so the answers to this quiz are on page 7. (Stop! Don't turn and look until you've done the quiz – they are there, we promise you!)

QUESTION 1
Who reached number one in 2014 with her single 'Crazy Stupid Love' (featuring Tinie Tempah)?

QUESTION 2
The duo Jon and Vangelis had two Top 10 singles at the beginning of the 1980s. Name either of them.

QUESTION 3
Who reached number one in 1969 with 'Israelites'?

QUESTION 4
Which 2002 number one by Gareth Gates has the subtitle '(Stupid Mistake)'?

QUESTION 5
Which group of comedians had a Top 10 hit in 1973 with 'Ying Tong Song'?

QUESTION 6
Which U2 song was a Top 3 hit for Mary J Blige with U2 in 2006?

QUESTION 7
What are the names of both of the members of the duo The Communards?

QUESTION 8
The 1991 single 'Radio Wall of Sound' was the final original Top 40 hit single for which group?

QUESTION 9
During the course of their chart career, the group Secret Affair had three Top 40 singles. Name one of them.

QUESTION 10
Who won the 'Best British Female Solo Artist' award at the 2015 BRIT Awards?

QUIZ 003 POPMASTER

Q1
Ike & Tina Turner

Q2
A Thing Called Love

Q3
Marc Almond

Q4
Have to Say You Love Me

Q5
'In Too Deep'

Q6
Stereophonics

Q7
'Hey Little Girl'

Q8
The Sweet

Q9
'Pink Cadillac' (No.5 in 1988), 'Miss You Like Crazy' (No.2 in 1989)

Q10
The Colourfield

QUESTION 1
Which group's number one singles in the 1960s included 'You Really Got Me' and 'Sunny Afternoon'?

QUESTION 2
The songs 'Forgive Me', 'Better in Time' and 'Happy' were all hits in the Noughties for which singer?

QUESTION 3
What shared one-word title has provided different Top 10 hits for Roy Orbison and Julee Cruise, a Top 20 hit for Ant & Dec and Top 40 hits for Cathy Dennis and McAlmont & Butler?

QUESTION 4
Which former American president featured in the title of a 2004 Top 3 single by Manic Street Preachers?

QUESTION 5
Who had hit cover versions in 1993 with the songs 'Ruby Tuesday', 'Shotgun Wedding' and 'Have I Told You Lately'?

QUESTION 6
Released in 1977, what is the title of the Steve Gibbons Band's only Top 40 hit?

QUESTION 7
What is the first name of the singer in Goldfrapp?

QUESTION 8
With whom did Sarah Brightman have a Top 3 hit in 1997 called 'Time to Say Goodbye (Con te Partiro)'?

QUESTION 9
The group Liverpool Express had three Top 40 hits in the mid-Seventies. Name one of them.

QUESTION 10
Which vocal group had Top 10 singles in 2006 called 'Whole Lotta History', 'Something Kinda Ooooh' and 'I Think We're Alone Now'?

POPMASTER QUIZ 004

QUESTION 1
Coldplay had their very first number one single in June 2008 – what was it called?

QUESTION 2
The song 'Happenin' All Over Again' was a Top 5 hit in 1990 for the American singer Lonnie… who?

QUESTION 3
In 1966, The Lovin' Spoonful had their only two Top 10 singles. Name one of them.

QUESTION 4
One of the most successful groups of the first half of the 1980s reached the Top 10 with 'Victims', 'The War Song' and 'It's a Miracle'. Who are they?

QUESTION 5
What was the title of the song by Rednex that spent three weeks at number one in 1995?

QUESTION 6
Songs sharing the title 'After the Love Has Gone' have provided different Top 40 hits for three chart acts – in 1979, 1985 and 1999. Name one of them.

QUESTION 7
What type of 'Divorce' did Steely Dan sing about on their 1976 single?

QUESTION 8
Which punk group has included Dave Vanian, Rat Scabies, Captain Sensible and Brian James amongst its line-up?

QUESTION 9
What is the title of the only Spice Girls number one to have the word 'Spice' in the title?

QUESTION 10
Which Liverpool group made its Top 40 debut in 1996 with 'Female of the Species'?

Q1
Cheryl Cole

Q2
'I Hear You Now', 'I'll Find My Way Home'

Q3
Desmond Dekker & The Aces

Q4
'Anyone of Us'

Q5
The Goons

Q6
'One'

Q7
Jimmy Somerville, Richard Coles

Q8
Slade

Q9
'Time for Action', 'Let Your Heart Dance', 'My World'

Q10
Paloma Faith

7

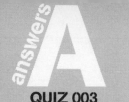

QUIZ 005 POPMASTER

Q1
The Kinks

Q2
Leona Lewis

Q3
'Falling'

Q4
Richard Nixon ('The Love of Richard Nixon')

Q5
Rod Stewart

Q6
'Tulane'

Q7
Alison

Q8
Andrea Bocelli

Q9
'You Are My Love', 'Every Man Must Have a Dream', 'Dreamin''

Q10
Girls Aloud

QUESTION 1
Which chart act reached number two in 1979 with the song 'Pop Muzik'?

QUESTION 2
Which Small Faces song did M People cover in 1995?

QUESTION 3
One of the most successful UK groups of the first half of the 1980s had a Top 10 double 'A' side in 1981 with 'Musclebound' and 'Glow'. Who are they?

QUESTION 4
Which American singer had hits in the mid-Fifties with the songs 'Indian Love Call', 'China Doll' and 'Tumbling Tumbleweeds'?

QUESTION 5
What one-word title has provided different hits for The Who in 1966 and 1976, Clout in 1978 and Liquid Gold in 1980?

QUESTION 6
Beginning with the earliest, put these three songs by Depeche Mode in the order they were originally hits: 'Personal Jesus', 'See You', 'Barrel of a Gun'?

QUESTION 7
What type of 'Rose' did Sting sing about in 2000 on his Top 20 single featuring raï singer Cheb Mami?

QUESTION 8
The 1980 Top 10 song 'You Gave Me Love' was recorded by Crown... what... Affair?

QUESTION 9
The songs 'My Sweet Rosalie', 'Oh Boy (The Mood I'm In)' and 'Beautiful Lover' were all hits in the Seventies for which vocal group?

QUESTION 10
Which of these 1960s singers is associated with the group The Dakotas – Johnny Kidd, Billy J Kramer or Freddie Garrity?

POPMASTER QUIZ 006

QUESTION 1
Which group made its chart debut in 1987 with the song 'Don't Dream It's Over'?

QUESTION 2
What shared one-word title has provided different hits for Rita Coolidge in 1978, F.R. David in 1983 and The Christians in 1989?

QUESTION 3
Which Australian singer reached the Top 10 in the early summer of 2008 with her single 'Sweet About Me'?

QUESTION 4
The theme tune to which Spaghetti Western film gave Hugo Montenegro, his Orchestra and Chorus a number one in 1968?

QUESTION 5
Name the American female country trio who made their UK chart debut in 1999 with the single 'There's Your Trouble'.

QUESTION 6
Two of the six Top 10 singles for Wizzard in the 1970s had the word 'Rock' somewhere in the title. Name one of these two songs.

QUESTION 7
What is the name of the male member of the duo Yazoo?

QUESTION 8
What do the chart acts The Honeycombs, Carpenters and The White Stripes have in common?

QUESTION 9
The 1986 debut hit for Mel & Kim had the subtitle '(Get Fresh at the Weekend)'. What was its full title?

QUESTION 10
The 1977 single 'Oh, Lori' was the only UK hit for which pair of American brothers?

Q1
'Viva la Vida'

Q2
Gordon

Q3
'Daydream', 'Summer in the City'

Q4
Culture Club

Q5
'Cotton Eye Joe'

Q6 *Earth Wind & Fire, Princess, Steps (Damage covered the EW&F song in 2001, but it stalled at No.42)*

Q7
Haitian

Q8
The Damned

Q9
'Spice Up Your Life'

Q10
Space

9

QUIZ 007 POPMASTER

Q1
M

Q2
'Itchycoo Park'

Q3
Spandau Ballet

Q4
Slim Whitman

Q5
'Substitute'

Q6
'See You' ('82), 'Personal Jesus' ('89), 'Barrel of a Gun' ('97)

Q7
'Desert Rose'

Q8
Heights

Q9
Brotherhood of Man

Q10
Billy J Kramer

QUESTION 1
Curt Smith is one of the two main members of Tears for Fears – who is the other?

QUESTION 2
Which of these three songs marked the chart debut of the group Toto – was it 'Africa', 'Hold the Line' or 'Rosanna'?

QUESTION 3
The singer who spent four weeks at number one in 1994 with 'Baby Come Back' is called Pato... who?

QUESTION 4
Name the American vocal group who had hits in the early 1970s with 'Didn't I (Blow Your Mind this Time)' and 'La-La Means I Love You'?

QUESTION 5
Which shared three-word title has provided different Top 40 hits for The Animals in 1965, Talk Talk in 1990, Dr Alban in 1992 and Bon Jovi in 2000?

QUESTION 6
Who had solo hits in the early 1980s called 'King's Call' and 'Yellow Pearl'?

QUESTION 7
Who am I? I was born in New Jersey in 1949, my songs have provided hits for Patti Smith, Manfred Mann's Earth Band and The Pointer Sisters, and my own number one albums include Devils & Dust and The Rising?

QUESTION 8
The Script had a Top 3 single in the Noughties called 'The Man Who Can't...' what?

QUESTION 9
Beginning with the earliest, put these three singles by David Bowie in the order they were originally hits: 'Hallo Spaceboy', 'Loving the Alien', 'Starman'?

QUESTION 10
Which politician featured in the video for Tracey Ullman's 1984 single 'My Guy'?

POPMASTER QUIZ 008

QUESTION 1
Which group reached the Top 5 in 1978 with the song 'With a Little Luck', taken from their Top 5 album London Town?

QUESTION 2
Complete the title of this 1981 single by Madness – 'The Return of the...' what?

QUESTION 3
The American group who had chart singles in the Noughties with 'Girl All the Bad Guys Want' and '1985' is called Bowling for... what?

QUESTION 4
George Harrison had three Top 40 solo hits in the 1980s – 'All Those Years Ago' was the first of these. Name one of the other two.

QUESTION 5
'Make it Easy on Yourself' was number one in 1965 for which group?

QUESTION 6
The group Razorlight had its only number one single in 2006 – what is it called?

QUESTION 7
Which of these groups had their only hit in 1983 with 'The Safety Dance'. Was it Roman Holliday, Men Without Hats or It's Immaterial?

QUESTION 8
What comes next in this sequence of albums released by Radiohead: Pablo Honey ('93), The Bends ('95), OK Computer ('97)...?

QUESTION 9
The American singer who had a hit in 1973 with 'Pillow Talk' had the same name as a Swedish singer who had a hit in 1974 with 'Y Viva Espana'. What is that shared name?

QUESTION 10
Released in 1982, which actor features in the title of the first and biggest hit for the duo Haysi Fantayzee?

Q1
Crowded House

Q2
'Words'

Q3
Gabriella Cilmi

Q4
'The Good, The Bad and The Ugly'

Q5
Dixie Chicks

Q6
'Rock 'N' Roll Winter (Loony's Tune), 'Are You Ready to Rock'

Q7
Vince Clarke

Q8
A female drummer

Q9
'Showing Out (Get Fresh at the Weekend)'

Q10
Alessi

QUIZ 007

Roland Orzabal

Q2
'Hold the Line' (1979; the other two are from 1983)

Q3
Banton

Q4
The Delfonics

Q5
'It's My Life'

Q6
Phil Lynott

Q7
Bruce Springsteen

Q8
Be Moved

Q9
'Starman' ('72), 'Loving the Alien' ('85), 'Hallo Spaceboy' ('96)

Q10
Neil Kinnock

QUIZ 009 POPMASTER

QUESTION 1
Which group had hits in 1978 with the songs 'Nice 'N' Sleazy' and '5 Minutes'?

QUESTION 2
According to Pat Benatar's 1985 Top 20 hit, 'Love is a...' what?

QUESTION 3
Who am I? Born Arnold Dorsey in 1936, my first three hits were in 1967, I recorded the Top 5 song 'Les Bicyclettes de Belsize' in '68 and I returned to the Top 40 in 1999 with 'Quando Quando Quando'. I represented the UK at Eurovision in 2012.

QUESTION 4
Beginning with the earliest, put these three songs by Kate Bush in the order they were originally hits: 'Moments of Pleasure', 'King of the Mountain' and 'Cloudbusting'?

QUESTION 5
One of the biggest UK groups of the early 1980s had their only Top 10 hit of the '90s in 1995 with 'Tell Me When'. Name the group.

QUESTION 6
What was the title of the 2002 number one by Nelly featuring Kelly Rowland?

QUESTION 7
In which decade did Cliff Richard have Top 10 singles with 'True Love Ways', 'Please Don't Fall in Love' and 'Daddy's Home'?

QUESTION 8
Which hit guitar-pop trio of the Noughties consisted of James Bourne, Charlie Simpson and Matt Willis?

QUESTION 9
The actor Bruce Willis had two Top 10 cover versions in 1987. Name one of them.

QUESTION 10
Which American vocal group's hits in the early Seventies included 'Elmo James', 'I'm on My Way to a Better Place' and 'Finders Keepers'?

12

POPMASTER QUIZ 010

QUESTION 1
Which 1969 single by The Who was also a chart hit in the Seventies for The New Seekers and Elton John?

QUESTION 2
Which one-time teen idol of the 1970s had his only Top 40 hit of the Eighties in 1985 with the Top 5 song 'The Last Kiss'?

QUESTION 3
What is the title of the 2014 number one song by Jessie J, Ariana Grande and Nicki Minaj?

QUESTION 4
Which group, featuring singer Miles Hunt, had Top 10 EPs in the early Nineties called 'Welcome to the Cheap Seats' and 'On the Ropes'?

QUESTION 5
Name the song originally by Wham! that gave Shane Richie a Top 3 single in 2003.

QUESTION 6
Fourteen years before their only UK number one, which American group made its chart debut in 1976 with the song 'Rock N' Me'?

QUESTION 7
In 1980, the Canadian group Rush had its biggest UK single with 'The Spirit of...' what?

QUESTION 8
The song 'This Kiss' was the 1998 chart debut by which American country singer?

QUESTION 9
In 1981, Fred Wedlock declared he was the 'Oldest... what... in Town'?

QUESTION 10
Although it failed to be a Top 40 hit, which American jazz instrumental group is best known for their 1977 single 'Birdland'?

Q1
Wings

Q2
Los Palmas Seven

Q3
Soup

Q4
'Got My Mind Set on You' ('87), 'When We was Fab' ('88)

Q5
The Walker Brothers

Q6
'America'

Q7
Men Without Hats

Q8
Kid A (2000)

Q9
Sylvia

Q10
John Wayne ('John Wayne is Big Leggy')

QUIZ 011 POPMASTER

Q1
The Stranglers

Q2
Battlefield

Q3
Engelbert Humperdinck

Q4
'Cloudbusting' ('85), 'Moments of Pleasure' ('93), 'King of the Mountain' (05)

Q5
Human League

Q6
'Dilemma'

Q7
1980s

Q8
Busted

Q9
'Respect Yourself', 'Under the Boardwalk'

Q10
The Chairmen of the Board

QUESTION 1
Which critically acclaimed American group is led by Donald Fagen and Walter Becker?

QUESTION 2
The American singer Lobo had two hits in the 1970s and both were Top 5 singles. Name either of them.

QUESTION 3
...and a Dutch singer also called Lobo had a Top 10 hit in 1981 with which song?

QUESTION 4
Which group had hits in 2004 with 'Matinee' and 'Michael'?

QUESTION 5
The songs 'Duel' and 'Dr Mabuse' were hits in the mid-1980s for Propaganda. Did the group come from The Netherlands, Germany or Sweden?

QUESTION 6
In 1992, Annie Lennox was 'Walking on...' what?

QUESTION 7
The Greek group Aphrodite's Child had its only UK hit in 1968 with 'Rain and Tears', but two of its members went on to have British solo success in the 1970s and 1980s. Name either of these members.

QUESTION 8
Which Beatles studio album includes the songs 'With a Little Help from My Friends', 'When I'm Sixty-Four', 'Lucy in the Sky with Diamonds' and 'Being for the Benefit of Mr Kite'?

QUESTION 9
In 1993, the film composer David Arnold had a hit with 'Play Dead' that featured vocals by which female singer?

QUESTION 10
The singer Curtis Stigers' first two chart singles were also his only Top 10 hits. Name either of these 1992 Top 10 songs.

POPMASTER QUIZ 012

QUESTION 1
Which singer-songwriter had both a hit single and album in 1980 called 'Me Myself I'?

QUESTION 2
With nearly three years in total on the chart, what was the title of the 1995 debut album by The Lighthouse Family that contained the singles 'Lifted', 'Goodbye Heartbreak' and 'Loving Every Minute'?

QUESTION 3
Which group was 'Bringing on Back the Good Times' in 1969?

QUESTION 4
What type of 'Weekend' did The Stylistics sing about on their 1976 Top 10 single?

QUESTION 5
Which American group released the number one albums Only by the Night in 2008, Come Around Sundown in 2010 and Mechanical Bull in 2014?

QUESTION 6
What nationality was the group Freiheit, who had a hit in the late Eighties with 'Keeping the Dream Alive' – were they German, Austrian or Swiss?

QUESTION 7
Who made her chart debut in 1978 with 'I'm Every Woman'?

QUESTION 8
Two of The Jam's hit singles had the word 'Town' somewhere in the title – 'Town Called Malice' was one, what was the other?

QUESTION 9
Which group had a Top 10 hit in 2007 with 'How to Save a Life'?

QUESTION 10
Having had three hits (including a number one) in 1979, which American vocal group began the 1980s with a Top 20 single called 'Can't Stop the Music'?

Q1 'Pinball Wizard' (The New Seekers' version paired the song with 'See Me, Feel Me' for a Top 20 medley)

Q2 David Cassidy

Q3 'Bang Bang'

Q4 The Wonder Stuff

Q5 'I'm Your Man'

Q6 Steve Miller Band

Q7 Radio

Q8 Faith Hill

Q9 Swinger

Q10 Weather Report

QUIZ 013 POPMASTER

Q1
Steely Dan

Q2
'Me and You and a Dog Named Boo', 'I'd Love You to Want Me'

Q3
'The Caribbean Disco Show'

Q4
Franz Ferdinand

Q5
Germany

Q6
Broken Glass

Q7
Demis Roussos, Vangelis

Q8
Sgt Pepper's Lonely Hearts Club Band

Q9
Björk

Q10
'I Wonder Why', 'You're All that Matters to Me'

QUESTION 1
The 2001 chart debut by Nelly Furtado was called 'I'm Like a...' what?

QUESTION 2
The 1996 Top 3 single 'If You Ever' was recorded as a duet by one of the most successful boy bands and one of the most successful British female singers of the time. Name either the boy band or the singer.

QUESTION 3
What song, written by George Gershwin with lyrics by DuBose Heyward, was taken into the chart in 1982 by Fun Boy Three?

QUESTION 4
The singer who reached number two in 1979 with 'Silly Games' is called Janet... who?

QUESTION 5
Which of Coldplay's albums contains the singles 'Shiver' and 'Trouble'?

QUESTION 6
What is the name of the drummer in U2?

QUESTION 7
The Queen songs 'Now I'm Here', 'Bicycle Race'/'Fat Bottomed Girls' and 'Save Me' all just missed the Top 10 by peaking at number 11, but which of these three singles was the first to make the chart?

QUESTION 8
Which American singer had a Top 30 hit in 1966 with 'Born a Woman' and a Top 20 hit in 1967 with 'Single Girl'?

QUESTION 9
What was the title of the 1997 chart debut by Finley Quaye?

QUESTION 10
Name the male vocalist who reached the Top 5 in 1983 with his single 'Calling Your Name'.

POPMASTER QUIZ 014

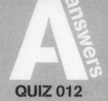
QUESTION 1
Who made her chart debut in 1973 with the song 'Can the Can'?

QUESTION 2
Characters from the TV series *The X Files* provided Catatonia with the title of their first Top 10 single in 1998. What was the song called?

QUESTION 3
The Australian group who had its only UK Top 40 hit in 1983 with the Top 10 song 'Waiting for a Train' is called Flash and… what?

QUESTION 4
The American vocal group The Tymes had two chart hits in the 1960s called 'So Much in Love' and 'People'. They had two further Top 40 hits in the 1970s. Name one of these.

QUESTION 5
Name the Canadian singer who made his debut on the singles chart in 2005 with the song 'Home', taken from his Top 5 album It's Time.

QUESTION 6
What type of '…Stomp' did Hamilton Bohannon sing about on his Top 10 hit in the mid-Seventies?

QUESTION 7
Who is the one-time lead singer with Japan who had solo hits in 1984 called 'Red Guitar' and 'The Ink in the Well'?

QUESTION 8
The Motown group Boyz II Men made its chart debut in 1992 with a song that spent three weeks at number one and five months on the chart. What is it called?

QUESTION 9
The 1986 single 'My Favourite Waste of Time' was the only hit single for which singer?

QUESTION 10
How do you pronounce the titles of the Ed Sheeran albums released in 2011 and 2014?

Q1
Joan Armatrading

Q2
Ocean Drive

Q3
Love Affair

Q4
'Funky Weekend'

Q5
Kings of Leon

Q6
German

Q7
Chaka Khan

Q8
'Strange Town'

Q9
The Fray

Q10
The Village People

17

QUIZ 015 POPMASTER

Q1
Bird

Q2
East 17, Gabrielle

Q3
'Summertime'

Q4
Kay

Q5
Parachutes

Q6
Larry Mullen Jr

Q7
'Now I'm Here'

Q8
Sandy Posey

Q9
'Sunday Shining'

Q10
Marilyn

QUESTION 1
Which American group made its debut Top 40 appearance in 1989 with the song 'Orange Crush'?

QUESTION 2
Which 1974 single by the Carpenters has the subtitle '(On the Bayou)'?

QUESTION 3
Who reached the Top 3 with her singles 'Don't be a Stranger' in 1993 and 'Escaping' in 1996?

QUESTION 4
Which shared five-word song title has provided different hits for Roxy Music in 1974, U2 in 1989, Bryan Adams in 1992 and 911 in 1998?

QUESTION 5
In 1983, in between Yazoo and Erasure, Vince Clarke reached the Top 5 with a song called 'Never Never', which featured Feargal Sharkey as vocalist. But under what name did they record this song?

QUESTION 6
Released in 2009, what is the title of the debut number one album by Florence + the Machine, which spent almost three years in the Top 75?

QUESTION 7
In 1980, the American musician Tom Browne reached the Top 10 with 'Funkin' for Jamaica (N.Y.)', but did he play saxophone, trumpet or trombone?

QUESTION 8
What is the name of Daniel Bedingfield's sister, who reached number one in 2004 with the song 'These Words'?

QUESTION 9
Name the group that had its only Top 40 hit in 1979 with 'Back of My Hand'.

QUESTION 10
The Associates made their only three Top 40 appearances in 1982. Name one of these three singles.

POPMASTER QUIZ 016

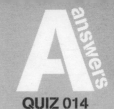

QUESTION 1
Name the Australian group that had hit singles in 1990 called 'Suicide Blonde' and 'Disappear', both taken from their hit album X.

QUESTION 2
The 1910 Fruitgum Co. made its only chart appearance in 1968 with a song that reached number two and spent four months on the chart - what was it called?

QUESTION 3
Having had a run of hits in the 1970s, which soul singer's only UK Top 40 hit of the 1980s was the 1987 single 'Sho' You Right'?

QUESTION 4
Released in 1976, the one and only hit for The Climax Blues Band was a Top 10 single in the autumn of that year - what was it called?

QUESTION 5
Which British female vocalist wanted to 'Keep this Fire Burning' in 2005?

QUESTION 6
Which American rapper, producer and entrepreneur had a number one soundtrack album in the summer of 2015 called Compton?

QUESTION 7
What was the title of the 1990 number one by Beats International featuring Lindy Layton that reworked a former SOS Band hit from 1984?

QUESTION 8
The song 'In a Lifetime' was a Top 20 hit in both 1986 and 1989 for Clannad. It featured guest vocals from the lead singer of another Irish band. Who was the guest vocalist?

QUESTION 9
Which instrument did Dave Clark play in The Dave Clark Five?

QUESTION 10
Was the 1978 Top 10 song 'Let's All Chant' the only hit for Narada Michael Walden, Michael Zager Band or Nick Straker Band?

Q1
Suzi Quatro

Q2
'Mulder and Scully'

Q3
The Pan

Q4
'You Little Trustmaker', 'Ms Grace'

Q5
Michael Bublé

Q6
'Disco Stomp'

Q7
David Sylvian

Q8
'End of the Road'

Q9
Owen Paul

Q10
Plus (+) Multiply (x)

19

Q1
R.E.M.

QUESTION 1
Brian Eno, Paul Thompson, Andy Mackay and Eddie Jobson have all been members of which group?

Q2
'Jambalaya'

QUESTION 2
The band Whitesnake had its only two UK Top 10 singles in 1987. Name either of them.

Q3
Dina Carroll

QUESTION 3
Which female vocal group had a Top 10 hit in 2014 with their cover version of Cameo's hit 'Word Up'?

Q4
'All I Want is You'

QUESTION 4
The 1970 number two song 'Patches' was the title of the only hit single for the American singer Clarence… who?

Q5
The Assembly

QUESTION 5
According to the title of their only Top 10 single in 1982, The Mobiles were doing what in Berlin?

Q6
Lungs

QUESTION 6
Name the American female vocal group whose British Top 10 singles in the 1990s included 'My Lovin'', 'Don't Let Go (Love)' and 'Hold On'.

Q7
Trumpet

QUESTION 7
What was the title of the 2010 Top 10 song by Enrique Iglesias that featured Nicole Scherzinger?

Q8
Natasha

QUESTION 8
Which band reached the Top 5 in 1989 with 'She Drives Me Crazy'?

Q9
The Jags

QUESTION 9
Which member of S Club 7 made her solo debut in 2005 with the Top 20 single 'What Hurts the Most'?

Q10 *'Party Fears Two',*
'Club Country', '18 Carat
Love Affair'/'Love Hangover'
(double 'A' side)

QUESTION 10
The Commodores reached the Top 3 in 1985 with a song that pays tribute to both Jackie Wilson and Marvin Gaye. What was it called?

POPMASTER QUIZ 018

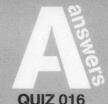

QUESTION 1
Which group was credited alongside Lloyd Cole on his recordings during the 1980s?

QUESTION 2
Beginning with the earliest, put these three songs by Elvis Presley in the order they were originally hits: 'All Shook Up', 'Moody Blue', 'Love Letters'.

QUESTION 3
A 1992 Top 10 version of Alice Cooper's '(I Want to be) Elected' was recorded by Mr Bean and Smear Campaign and featured which rock vocalist?

QUESTION 4
What was the title of the 1986 Top 3 duet by Patti LaBelle and Michael McDonald?

QUESTION 5
Which British rock group had a Top 3 single in 1995 called 'When Love and Hate Collide'?

QUESTION 6
Released in 1969 and 1970, which group's last Top 10 single of the Sixties was 'Viva Bobby Joe' and first of the Seventies 'Black Skin Blue Eyed Boys'?

QUESTION 7
The American vocal group The Whispers had their two UK Top 10 singles in the early 1980s. Name either of them.

QUESTION 8
'King' is the title of a 2015 number one by a London-based electronica band fronted by Olly Alexander. What is the band called?

QUESTION 9
Which 1996 Top 10 single by Radiohead has the subtitle '(Fade Out)'?

QUESTION 10
Barbra Streisand's 1988 Top 20 duet 'Till I Loved You (Love Theme from 'Goya')' was recorded with an actor from one of the most successful American TV series of the Eighties. Who is he?

Q1
INXS

Q2
'Simon Says'

Q3
Barry White

Q4
'Couldn't Get it Right'

Q5
Beverley Knight

Q6
Dr Dre

Q7
'Dub be Good to Me' (the original SOS Band hit was called 'Just be Good to Me')

Q8
Bono (U2)

Q9
Drums

Q10
Michael Zager Band

21

QUIZ 019 POPMASTER

Q1
Roxy Music

Q2
'Is this Love, 'Here I Go Again' (re-mix)

Q3
Little Mix (recorded for Sport Relief)

Q4
Carter

Q5
'Drowning in Berlin'

Q6
En Vogue

Q7
'Heartbeat'

Q8
Fine Young Cannibals

Q9
Jo O'Meara

Q10
'Nightshift'

QUESTION 1
Who had hits in 1986 with the singles 'What Have You Done for Me Lately', 'Nasty' and 'When I Think of You'?

QUESTION 2
Which 2014 number one by Clean Bandit featuring Jess Glynne has become a musical favourite of advertising companies?

QUESTION 3
Which Scottish group had hits in the 1990s with 'Nothing Ever Happens', 'Always the Last to Know' and 'Driving with the Brakes On'?

QUESTION 4
The 1984 hit duet by Julio Iglesias and Willie Nelson was called 'To All the…' what?

QUESTION 5
Name the American vocal group who sang about 'The Rubberband Man' in 1976?

QUESTION 6
One of the final original hits for ABBA mentions the author Marilyn French, Chinese food and the TV series *Dallas* in its lyrics. What is it called?

QUESTION 7
Which group had Top 10 singles in 1964 with 'Just One Look', 'Here I Go Again' and 'We're Through'?

QUESTION 8
The Swiss duo Double reached the Top 10 in 1986 with their only Top 40 hit single. What was it called?

QUESTION 9
The songs 'Skinny Genes' and 'Pack Up' were hits in 2010 for the daughter of West End star Frances Ruffelle and granddaughter of Sylvia Young, founder of the famous theatre school. Who is she?

QUESTION 10
Which two drinks featured in the title of Dr Feelgood's 1979 Top 10 single?

POPMASTER QUIZ 020

QUESTION 1
Which song by Ian Dury & The Blockheads mentions the Marx Brothers, a hit song by Little Richard and the director of the film *Annie Hall* in its lyrics?

QUESTION 2
Which band had hits in the mid '90s called 'Staying out for the Summer' and 'Good Enough'?

QUESTION 3
Which early Eighties hit for Leo Sayer was written by Barry and Robin Gibb and produced by Arif Mardin?

QUESTION 4
Brothers Howard and Guy Lawrence released a number one album called Settle in 2013 and had a Top 20 single in 2015 with 'Omen', which featured vocals by Sam Smith. Under what name do the brothers record?

QUESTION 5
Manfred Mann's Paul Jones had two solo Top 10 singles in the 1960s. Name either of them.

QUESTION 6
Which group of the early 1980s had its final Top 40 hits in 1983 with the songs 'Don't Talk to Me About Love' and 'Bring Me Closer'?

QUESTION 7
Christina Aguilera made her chart debut in 1999 with her first number one single. What was it called?

QUESTION 8
'Bonfire Heart' was a Top 5 single in 2013 for which singer-songwriter?

QUESTION 9
What is the title of the Top 3 single from 2000 credited to Tom Jones and Mousse T?

QUESTION 10
Having had success with three different chart groups, who had solo hit singles in 1973 with 'Dear Elaine' and 'Forever'?

Q1
The Commotions

Q2
'All Shook Up' ('57), 'Love Letters' ('66), 'Moody Blue' ('77)

Q3
Bruce Dickinson

Q4
'On My Own'

Q5
Def Leppard

Q6
The Equals

Q7
'And the Beat Goes On', 'It's a Love Thing'

Q8
Years & Years

Q9
'Street Spirit'

Q10
Don Johnson (from Miami Vice)

QUIZ 019

Q1
Janet Jackson

Q2
'Rather Be'

Q3
Del Amitri

Q4
Girls I've Loved Before

Q5
The Detroit Spinners

Q6
'The Day Before You Came'

Q7
The Hollies

Q8
'The Captain of Her Heart'

Q9
Eliza Doolittle

Q10
'Milk and Alcohol'

QUESTION 1
Which Swedish group's hits in the 1990s included 'Happy Nation', 'Always Have, Always Will' and 'Life is a Flower'?

QUESTION 2
What was the title of Owl City's 2010 number one debut hit?

QUESTION 3
Who am I? I had my first hits as a member of the American teen group New Edition in 1983, my first UK Top 10 song was a 1988 release called 'My Prerogative', and I married Whitney Houston in 1992?

QUESTION 4
Name the Ray Davies song released as part of a double 'A' side single with "'A' Bomb in Wardour Street" by The Jam in 1978.

QUESTION 5
What type of 'Game' did Chris Isaak sing about on his 1990 chart debut?

QUESTION 6
Name two of the three members of A-ha.

QUESTION 7
'Ring out Solstice Bells' was a Christmas hit in 1976 for which folk-rock group?

QUESTION 8
Which U2 single from the Eighties featured a guest appearance from B.B. King?

QUESTION 9
The 1978 single 'I Love the Nightlife (Disco 'Round)' was the only Top 40 hit for the American singer Alicia... who?

QUESTION 10
What was the title of The Script's 2012 number one that featured will.i.am?

POPMASTER QUIZ 022

QUESTION 1
What was the title of the 1986 chart debut by Bruce Hornsby & The Range?

QUESTION 2
Which of these chart acts reached the Top 10 in 1978 with 'Supernature' – was it Eruption, Cerrone or Crown Heights Affair?

QUESTION 3
In 1994, the duo Corona spent 18 weeks on the chart and reached number two with 'The Rhythm of…' what?

QUESTION 4
Which British singer-songwriter had hits in the first half of the 1970s with 'Getting a Drag', 'Sugar Me' and 'Won't Somebody Dance with Me'?

QUESTION 5
Craig David had a Top 3 hit in 2003 with a song that featured Sting as a guest vocalist – what was it called?

QUESTION 6
The American singer who had his only two UK hits in 1980 with 'Escape (The Pina Colada Song)' and 'Him' is called Rupert… ?

QUESTION 7
What was Robin Gibb 'Saved by…', according to the title of his 1969 solo hit?

QUESTION 8
What was the surname of Mac and Katie, who had hits in 1975 with 'Sugar Candy Kisses', 'Don't Do it Baby' and 'Like a Butterfly'?

QUESTION 9
In 1985, David Grant and Jaki Graham had a Top 5 hit with a cover of a Detroit Spinners hit from 1973. What was it called?

QUESTION 10
Released in 2005, which member of Blue began his solo career with the Top 5 singles 'Lay Your Hands' and 'No Worries'?

Q1
'Reasons to be Cheerful (Pt.3)'

Q2
Dodgy

Q3
'Heart (Stop Beating in Time)'

Q4
Disclosure

Q5
'High Time', 'I've Been a Bad, Bad Boy'

Q6
Altered Images

Q7
'Genie in a Bottle'

Q8
James Blunt

Q9
'Sex Bomb'

Q10
Roy Wood (The Move, ELO's '10538 Overture', Wizzard)

QUIZ 023 POPMASTER

Q1
Ace of Base

Q2
'Fireflies'

Q3
Bobby Brown

Q4
David Watts

Q5
'Wicked Game'

Q6 *Morten Harket, Pal Waaktaar (now known as Paul Waaktaar-Savoy, Magne Furuholmen ('Mags')*

Q7
Jethro Tull

Q8
'When Love Comes to Town'

Q9
Bridges

Q10
'Hall of Fame'

QUESTION 1
'Suedehead' is the title of the 1988 debut solo single by which artist?

QUESTION 2
The American rock band Boston reached the singles chart in 1977 with the song 'More than a...' what?

QUESTION 3
Which group had hits in 2012 called 'Survival' and 'Madness' – both taken from their number one album The 2nd Law?

QUESTION 4
Which James Bond theme song was covered by Guns N' Roses for a Top 5 hit in 1991?

QUESTION 5
The group that had all three of its Top 40 hits in 1980, with 'Living by Numbers', 'This World of Water' and 'Sanctuary', was called New... what?

QUESTION 6
Which 1968 hit for Union Gap featuring Gary Puckett reached the chart again in 1974, but this time credited as Gary Puckett and the Union Gap?

QUESTION 7
Which singer comes next in this sequence – Steve Brookstein, Shayne Ward, Leona Lewis, Leon Jackson... ?

QUESTION 8
...and what is the name of the only group to win the UK version of *The X Factor* in the first 10 years of its run?

QUESTION 9
The songs 'You're Lying' and 'Intuition' were hits at the start of the 1980s for which of these groups – Beggar and Co, Linx or Loose Ends?

QUESTION 10
Name the EastEnders actress who had hits in the 1990s with 'Looking Up', 'Happy Just to be with You' and 'Do You Know'.

POPMASTER QUIZ 024

QUESTION 1
Graham Gouldman and Lol Creme were two of the four members of the original 10cc. Who were the other two?

QUESTION 2
Released in 1979, what was the title of the first and biggest hit for the group Sad Cafe?

QUESTION 3
Which family group released albums in the 1990s called Forgiven Not Forgotten and Talk on Corners?

QUESTION 4
What word appears in the titles of different hit singles in the Seventies by The Goodies, Wild Cherry and KC & The Sunshine Band?

QUESTION 5
Which Nashville group had a Top 30 hit in 2010 and a Top 20 hit in 2012 with the song 'Need You Now'?

QUESTION 6
The group Mr Mister had two hit singles in the mid-Eighties. Name either of them.

QUESTION 7
Name the soul singer who had hits in 1966 with 'Fa Fa Fa Fa Fa (Sad Song)' and a cover of '(I Can't Get No) Satisfaction' and a posthumous hit in 1968 with 'Hard to Handle'.

QUESTION 8
In the summer of 2008, The Ting Tings had a Top 10 single called 'Shut Up and…' what?

QUESTION 9
What do the initials 'PJ' stand for in PJ Harvey?

QUESTION 10
The duo Candy Flip had its only Top 40 hit in 1990 with a Top 3 cover version of which Beatles song?

Q1
'The Way it Is'

Q2
Cerrone

Q3
'The Rhythm of the Night'

Q4
Lynsey De Paul

Q5
'Rise & Fall'

Q6
Holmes

Q7
'Saved by the Bell'

Q8
Kissoon

Q9
'Could it Be I'm Falling in Love'

Q10
Simon Webbe

QUIZ 025 POPMASTER

Q1
Morrissey

Q2
'More than a Feeling'

Q3
Muse

Q4
'Live and Let Die'

Q5
Musik

Q6
'Young Girl'

Q7
Alexandra Burke (the first five winners of The X Factor, from 2004 to 2008)

Q8
Little Mix (2011)

Q9
Linx

Q10
Michelle Gayle

QUESTION 1
Who wrote all of the hit singles by the American group Bread?

QUESTION 2
What is the title of the 1984 Top 3 single by Giorgio Moroder and Phil Oakey?

QUESTION 3
Name the Danish group that had its biggest UK hit in 2008 with 'Fascination', but has also had hits with '10,000 Nights of Thunder', 'Boyfriend' and 'The Spell'.

QUESTION 4
Lenny Kravitz had his only number one single in 1999 – what was it called?

QUESTION 5
Which of these groups had a Top 20 hit in 1983 with the song 'Don't Try to Stop It' – Halo James, Roman Holliday or Jo Boxers?

QUESTION 6
What were OneRepublic 'Counting…' according to the title of their 2013 number one?

QUESTION 7
What are the names of the two members of Roxette?

QUESTION 8
The group 5000 Volts had two hits in the mid-1970s. Name either of them.

QUESTION 9
Having had Top 10 hits in the Sixties, Seventies and Eighties, which group had further Top 10 singles in the Nineties with 'Secret Love', 'Alone' and 'For Whom the Bell Tolls'?

QUESTION 10
Two hit singles in 2004 by Scissor Sisters had female names as their titles – name both of them.

POPMASTER QUIZ 026

QUESTION 1
What are the first names of the two Everly Brothers?

QUESTION 2
The singer Fontella Bass had her biggest hit with a song that reached the chart in 1965. What is it called?

QUESTION 3
Jazzie B is the founder, leader and producer of which British hit group of the Eighties and Nineties?

QUESTION 4
What was the title of David Essex's 1973 chart debut?

QUESTION 5
Which group reached the Top 10 in 2008 singing about 'Violet Hill'?

QUESTION 6
What was 'Kinky...', according to the title of the Happy Mondays' 1990 Top 5 single?

QUESTION 7
'Into the Blue' was a Top 20 hit in 2014 for which Australian singer?

QUESTION 8
What word appears in the titles of different hit singles by Emerson Lake & Palmer, Paul Young and Pulp?

QUESTION 9
Who comes next in this sequence of artists – The New Seekers, Cliff Richard, Olivia Newton-John, The Shadows... ?

QUESTION 10
The 1989 Top 10 duet 'Wait' was recorded by Kym Mazelle along with the lead singer of The Blow Monkeys. What is he called?

Q1
Kevin Godley, Eric Stewart

Q2
'Everyday Hurts' (produced and engineered by Eric Stewart of 10cc)

Q3
The Corrs

Q4
Funky ('Funky Gibbon', 'Play that Funky Music', 'Sound Your Funky Horn')

Q5
Lady Antebellum

Q6
'Broken Wings', 'Kyrie' (both No.1 in the USA)

Q7
Otis Redding

Q8
'Shut Up and Let Me Go'

Q9
Polly Jean

Q10
'Strawberry Fields Forever'

QUIZ 027 POPMASTER

Q1
David Gates

Q2
'Together in Electric Dreams'

Q3
Alphabeat

Q4
'Fly Away'

Q5
Roman Holliday

Q6
Stars

Q7
Per Gessle, Marie Fredriksson

Q8
'I'm on Fire', 'Doctor Kiss-Kiss'

Q9
Bee Gees

Q10
'Laura', 'Mary'

QUESTION 1
Both of the lead singers with Genesis in the 1970s have also had successful solo careers. Name both of them.

QUESTION 2
'Billy-Ray' was the subject of the lyrics of Dusty Springfield's final Top 10 hit of the 1960s. What was it called?

QUESTION 3
One of the most successful UK groups of the Noughties consisted of Tom Fletcher, Danny Jones, Dougie Poynter and Harry Judd. Name the group.

QUESTION 4
What one word has provided the title for different hit songs by Tears for Fears in 1983, Lisa Stansfield in 1991 and The Lightning Seeds in 1995?

QUESTION 5
Which American band made its debut on the UK singles chart in 2012 with 'Radioactive', taken from their album Night Visions, a Top 3 hit in 2013?

QUESTION 6
Which group had hits in the mid-Seventies with 'Only You Can', 'Imagine Me Imagine You' and 'S-S-S-Single Bed'?

QUESTION 7
Which Rolling Stones song gave Susan Boyle a Top 10 single in December 2009?

QUESTION 8
Name the American singer who had Top 10 hits in the '90s called 'Breathe Again', 'Un-Break My Heart' and 'I Don't Want To'.

QUESTION 9
Leapy Lee had 'Little…' ones, ABC had a 'Poison…' one, and Pixie Lott had a 'Broken…' one. What are they?

QUESTION 10
'Take Me to the Mardi Gras' was a hit in 1973 for which American singer-songwriter?

POPMASTER QUIZ 028

QUESTION 1
Which influential Manchester band had Top 10 singles in 1990 with 'Elephant Stone' and 'One Love'?

QUESTION 2
The 2002 debut hit by Darius was also the singer's only number one single – what was it called?

QUESTION 3
Which group had hits in the first half of the Seventies with 'One and One is One', 'Rising Sun' and 'Slip and Slide'?

QUESTION 4
The American group Mr Big had its biggest hit in 1992 with a song that was Top 3 in the UK and number one in the States. What is it called?

QUESTION 5
Prior to announcing a group hiatus, which member of One Direction reduced the group from a five-piece to a quartet?

QUESTION 6
Which group sang about a 'Honaloochie Boogie' in 1973?

QUESTION 7
Who was the lead singer with The Stranglers during the 1970s and 1980s?

QUESTION 8
Released in 2010 and 2012, Ellie Goulding's first two albums both reached number one. Name either of them.

QUESTION 9
Who was Nile Rodgers' writing and production partner on hits for Sister Sledge, Chic, Diana Ross and Sheila & B. Devotion?

QUESTION 10
When The Beatles' Anthology series was released in the mid-'90s, two John Lennon songs were reworked by the remaining Beatles with co-producer Jeff Lynne and released as singles. Name either of these Top 5 hits.

Q1
Phil, Don

Q2
'Rescue Me'

Q3
Soul II Soul

Q4
'Rock On'

Q5
Coldplay

Q6
Afro

Q7
Kylie Minogue

Q8 *Common ('Fanfare for the Common Man', 'Love of the Common People', 'Common People')*

Q9
Brotherhood of Man (UK Eurovision Song Contest entries, 1972-1976)

Q10
Robert Howard (known as Dr Robert in The Blow Monkeys)

31

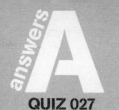

QUIZ 029 POPMASTER

Q1
Peter Gabriel, Phil Collins

Q2
'Son of a Preacher Man'

Q3
McFly

Q4
'Change'

Q5
Imagine Dragons

Q6
Fox

Q7
'Wild Horses'

Q8
Toni Braxton

Q9
Arrows ('Little Arrows', 'Poison Arrow', 'Broken Arrow')

Q10
Paul Simon

QUESTION 1
Talking Heads made their UK singles chart debut in 1981 with the song 'Once in a...' what?

QUESTION 2
The 2001 Top 5 song 'Nobody Wants to be Lonely' was recorded by Ricky Martin and which American female singer?

QUESTION 3
What girls name provided the title of Blondie's 1999 comeback number one single?

QUESTION 4
The 1979 single 'King Rocker' was the biggest hit for a group that featured Billy Idol as lead singer. What were they called?

QUESTION 5
Gordon Haskell made his only Top 40 appearance with a 2001 song that reached number two. What was it called?

QUESTION 6
The group Freeez had two Top 10 singles in the early 1980s. Name either of them.

QUESTION 7
Which Canadian singer reached number one in 2006 with her single 'Maneater'?

QUESTION 8
What was '...in Your Soul', according to the title of the 1990 Top 10 single by They Might be Giants?

QUESTION 9
The songs 'All of Me Loves All of You', 'Summerlove Sensation' and 'Love Me Like I Love You' were all Top 10 songs in the mid-1970s for which group?

QUESTION 10
Black Sabbath had a number one album in 1970 with Paranoid, the group's second studio album. Their next number one album came in 2013 with their 19th studio album. What was this album called?

POPMASTER QUIZ 030

QUESTION 1
Which American city features in the title of songs in the Seventies by T.Rex, Hello and Darts?

QUESTION 2
The 2006 hits 'You Give Me Something', 'Wonderful World' and 'The Pieces Don't Fit Anymore' all featured on the number one album Undiscovered by which singer-songwriter?

QUESTION 3
Released in 1983, which Top 10 single by Mike Oldfield featured vocals by Maggie Reilly?

QUESTION 4
Who sang about 'Galveston' in 1969?

QUESTION 5
What was the one-word title of the 1995 Top 3 duet by Michael Jackson and Janet Jackson?

QUESTION 6
Who released Top 5 albums in 2011 called Director's Cut and 50 Words for Snow?

QUESTION 7
Released in 1975, what is the title of the only Top 10 single by Pete Wingfield?

QUESTION 8
Who comes next in this sequence – Tina Turner, Sheryl Crow, Garbage, Madonna... ?

QUESTION 9
The Housemartins had a number one single during their chart career in the 1980s. What was it called?

QUESTION 10
Name the Scottish group that had hits in the mid-1970s with 'This Flight Tonight', 'Bad Bad Boy' and 'My White Bicycle'.

Q1
The Stone Roses

Q2
'Colourblind'

Q3
Medicine Head

Q4
'To be with You'

Q5
Zayn Malik

Q6
Mott the Hoople

Q7
Hugh Cornwell

Q8
Lights ('10), Halcyon ('12)

Q9
Bernard Edwards

Q10
'Free as a Bird', 'Real Love'

QUIZ 031 POPMASTER

Q1
Lifetime

Q2
Christina Aguilera

Q3
'Maria'

Q4
Generation X

Q5
'How Wonderful You Are'

Q6
'Southern Freeez', 'I.O.U.'

Q7
Nelly Furtado

Q8
Birdhouse

Q9
Bay City Rollers

Q10
13

QUESTION 1
Which hit by The Beatles that topped the chart for six weeks in 1969 credited Billy Preston on the label?

QUESTION 2
Can you name the singer who first made the top forty in 1993 with 'Caught in the Middle' who then reached the top twenty the following year after being re-mixed?

QUESTION 3
'No More (Baby I'ma do Right)' was a top ten hit in 2001 for which American vocal group?

QUESTION 4
Can you name the singer whose second of four top forty hits from 2005 was titled 'Other Side of the World'?

QUESTION 5
Which 1969 top twenty hit by Jackie Wilson was successfully re-issued in 1975 as part of a double 'A' side with 'I Get the Sweetest Feeling'?

QUESTION 6
Who topped the UK singles chart in 2015 with a song called 'Marvin Gaye' that featured vocals by Meghan Trainor?

QUESTION 7
Can you name the act that topped the chart for four weeks in 1995 with 'Boom Boom Boom'?

QUESTION 8
In 1969, after achieving two top ten hits, which group just failed to make the top forty with 'Are You Growing Tired of My Love', but later went on to have dozens more hits?

QUESTION 9
What is the title of the song that was a top twenty hit in 1964 for The Ronettes and a top ten hit in 1980 for the Ramones?

QUESTION 10
Which famous actor joins Sharleen Spiteri and Texas in the video for their 2000 top ten hit song 'In Demand'?

POPMASTER QUIZ 032

QUESTION 1
'Running Bear' was one of two top three hits for Johnny Preston in 1960. What was the other?

QUESTION 2
Who topped the chart for the fourth time with his 2011 single 'The Lazy Song'?

QUESTION 3
Can you name the duo who recorded the 1975 top ten hit 'Blue Guitar'?

QUESTION 4
Can you name the Spanish singer who topped the singles chart for four weeks in 2002 with 'Hero'?

QUESTION 5
Which group took Dan Hartman's 1978 top ten hit 'Instant Replay' back into the chart in 1990?

QUESTION 6
What song title is shared by a top ten hit from 1983 by Musical Youth and a 1987 number one by Rick Astley?

QUESTION 7
According to Lieutenant Pigeon's 1972 number one hit, what was 'Mouldy'?

QUESTION 8
Can you name the group that topped the chart in 2010 with 'This Ain't a Love Song'?

QUESTION 9
Which legendary female singer achieved top five hits in the Fifties with 'Mr Wonderful' and 'Fever'?

QUESTION 10
Can you name the crooner who made the top ten in 1962 with a song called 'Softly as I Leave You'?

Q1
New York ('New York City', 'New York Groove', 'Boy from New York City')

Q2
James Morrison

Q3
'Moonlight Shadow'

Q4
Glen Campbell

Q5
'Scream'

Q6
Kate Bush

Q7
'Eighteen with a Bullet'

Q8
Chris Cornell (James Bond theme songs, 1997-2006)

Q9
'Caravan of Love'

Q10
Nazareth

QUIZ 033 POPMASTER

Q1
'Get Back'

Q2
Juliet Roberts

Q3
3LW

Q4
KT Tunstall

Q5
'(Your Love Keeps Lifting Me) Higher and Higher'

Q6
Charlie Puth

Q7
The Outhere Brothers

Q8
Status Quo

Q9
'Baby, I Love You'

Q10
Alan Rickman

QUESTION 1
From 1973, what was the title of the only top five hit by The Hotshots that was a cover of the original 1967 hit by The Royal Guardsmen?

QUESTION 2
Can you name the Andrew Lloyd Webber and Tim Rice musical that provided Boyzone with their 1998 chart-topping single 'No Matter What'?

QUESTION 3
Petula Clark achieved two number one hits in the Sixties. The first was called 'Sailor', but what was the title of the other?

QUESTION 4
Can you name the singer who topped the chart in 2011 with his hit single 'Dance with Me Tonight'?

QUESTION 5
In 1980, which duo topped the American chart and achieved their only UK top ten hit with 'Do that to Me One More Time'?

QUESTION 6
Which female singer achieved a top twenty hit in 1997 with the title song to the James Bond movie *Tomorrow Never Dies*?

QUESTION 7
Which rock band topped the albums chart in 1992 with Automatic for the People?

QUESTION 8
According to her 1993 top ten hit, which female singer was looking in 'All the Right Places'?

QUESTION 9
In 1985, Aled Jones reached the top ten with the song 'Walking in the Air' that came from which famous animated movie?

QUESTION 10
What was the title of Paul Simon's first solo top five hit in 1972 after his break-up with Art Garfunkel?

POPMASTER QUIZ 034

QUESTION 1
Which legendary rock and roll singer scored a top twenty hit in 1961 with a song called 'Weekend'?

QUESTION 2
Shakatak scored two top ten hits in the Eighties. The first was 'Night Birds', but what was the title of the other?

QUESTION 3
What song title is shared by a top ten hit from 1973 by The O'Jays and a 1989 top five hit by Holly Johnson?

QUESTION 4
Under what name did British male producer Dave Lee release 'American Dream', his mainly instrumental debut top three hit from 2001?

QUESTION 5
Can you name the group that topped the chart in 1976 with 'Forever and Ever' and included Midge Ure in their line-up?

QUESTION 6
From 1969, Zager and Evans became the only duo to date whose name begins with a 'Z' to top both the UK and American charts. What was the title of their number one hit?

QUESTION 7
Can you name the female vocal group that made their chart debut in 2008 with 'If This is Love'?

QUESTION 8
What was the title of the 1999 top twenty hit by The Three Amigos that was also featured in the movie *American Pie*?

QUESTION 9
Who wrote the 1982 top twenty hit 'Ziggy Stardust', by Northampton group Bauhaus?

QUESTION 10
In 1969, which group achieved the last of their four top twenty hits with 'In the Bad Bad Old Days (Before You Loved Me)'?

Q1
'Cradle of Love'

Q2
Bruno Mars

Q3
Justin Hayward and John Lodge

Q4
Enrique Iglesias

Q5
Yell!

Q6
'Never Gonna Give You Up'

Q7
Old Dough

Q8
Scouting for Girls

Q9
Peggy Lee

Q10
Matt Monro

QUIZ 035 POPMASTER

Q1
'Snoopy vs The Red Baron'

Q2
Whistle Down the Wind

Q3
'This is My Song'

Q4
Olly Murs

Q5
Captain and Tennille

Q6
Sheryl Crow

Q7
R.E.M.

Q8
Lisa Stansfield

Q9
The Snowman

Q10
'Mother and Child Reunion'

QUESTION 1
Australian group The Easybeats achieved two top twenty hits in the Sixties – the first was 'Friday on My Mind', but what was the title of the other song?

QUESTION 2
Which successful act made the top ten in 2004 with their hit single 'Comfortably Numb'?

QUESTION 3
Can you name the group that achieved a top ten hit in 1971 with 'What are You Doing Sunday'?

QUESTION 4
Which band made their 1990 top forty chart debut with 'The Groovy Train'?

QUESTION 5
Which Birmingham ska band made their 1979 top ten chart debut with the double 'A'-sided hit 'Tears of a Clown' and 'Ranking Full Stop'?

QUESTION 6
Can you name the female singer who topped the chart in 2013 with 'We Can't Stop'?

QUESTION 7
From 1988, which group achieved their 11th top forty hit with 'King of Emotion'?

QUESTION 8
In which 1962 movie did Elvis Presley first feature his double 'A'-sided number one hits 'Rock-a-Hula-Baby' and 'Can't Help Falling in Love'?

QUESTION 9
According to their 1980 top ten hit, which legendary group experienced an 'Emotional Rescue'?

QUESTION 10
Can you name the American rock band that made the top five in 2001 with a cover of Erasure's 1988 hit 'A Little Respect'?

POPMASTER QUIZ 036

QUESTION 1
According to her 2008 top twenty hit, which female singer gave us the 'Cold Shoulder'?

QUESTION 2
From 1960, can you name the only top ten hit achieved by the Danish husband and wife duo Nina and Frederik?

QUESTION 3
American group The Manhattans scored two top ten hits in 1976 – the first was 'Kiss and Say Goodbye', but what was the title of the other hit?

QUESTION 4
In 2005, which female singer made the top five with 'Nine Million Bicycles'?

QUESTION 5
From 1980, what was the title of the only top forty hit by Australian duo Air Supply?

QUESTION 6
'Black or White' by Michael Jackson topped both the UK and American charts in 1991, but which famous musician was featured playing the guitar solo?

QUESTION 7
Which Swiss singer and songwriter scored a top twenty hit in 1978 with 'I Love America'?

QUESTION 8
According to their 1991 number two hit, which group climbed aboard the 'Last Train to Trancentral'?

QUESTION 9
In which 1962 movie did Elvis Presley first feature his number one hit 'Return to Sender'?

QUESTION 10
Can you name the British group that made their top ten chart debut in 2004 with 'Pressure Point...'?

Q1
Eddie Cochran

Q2
'Down on the Street'

Q3
'Love Train'

Q4
Jakatta

Q5
Slik

Q6
'In the Year 2525 (Exordium and Terminus)'

Q7
The Saturdays

Q8
'Louie Louie'

Q9
David Bowie

Q10
The Foundations

QUIZ 037 POPMASTER

Q1
'Hello, How Are You'

Q2
Scissor Sisters

Q3
Dawn featuring Tony Orlando

Q4
The Farm

Q5
The Beat

Q6
Miley Cyrus

Q7
Big Country

Q8
Blue Hawaii

Q9
The Rolling Stones

Q10
Wheatus

QUESTION 1
In what year did Go West make their chart debut with 'We Close Our Eyes'?

QUESTION 2
Which group achieved two top ten hits in 1998 with 'Come Back to What You Know' and 'My Weakness is None of Your Business'?

QUESTION 3
In 1985, which singer, songwriter and drummer's ninth solo top twenty hit was titled 'Take Me Home'?

QUESTION 4
Can you remember the title of the song by Geraldine – aka Peter Kay – that crashed into the chart at number two in 2008?

QUESTION 5
In 1993, a single by Take That featuring Lulu entered the chart at number one. Can you remember the title?

QUESTION 6
Desmond Dekker & The Aces topped the singles chart in 1969 with 'Israelites', and the follow-up also made the top ten. Can you name it?

QUESTION 7
Can you name the group that reached the top three in 1984 mainly due to the popularity of their record 'Agadoo' in holiday resorts abroad?

QUESTION 8
Apart from their number one with Baddiel & Skinner, can you name the only other single by The Lightning Seeds to make the top ten in the Nineties?

QUESTION 9
Can you name the group that achieved a number one album in 1969 with On the Threshold of a Dream?

QUESTION 10
Which singer topped the chart for four weeks in 2003 with his single 'Ignition'?

POPMASTER QUIZ 038

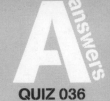
QUESTION 1
Which legendary easy listening singer achieved his last solo top twenty hit of the Seventies with the disco-flavoured 'Gone, Gone, Gone'?

QUESTION 2
Can you name the group that had their first UK top ten hit in 1995 with 'I've Got a Little Something for You'?

QUESTION 3
In 1995, and with the help of Vic Reeves and Bob Mortimer, which group successfully revived The Monkees' 1967 chart-topper 'I'm a Believer'?

QUESTION 4
Can you name the group that made the top twenty in 1981 with 'Sgt Rock (Is Going to Help Me)'?

QUESTION 5
Which female singer reached the top twenty in 1973 with her version of John Denver's song 'Take Me Home Country Roads'?

QUESTION 6
In 1985, German keyboard player Harold Faltermeyer reached number two in the chart with 'Axel F', but can you name the group that took the song back into the top ten in 1995?

QUESTION 7
In 1980, The Jam scored a double 'A'-sided number one hit. 'Going Underground' was on one side, but what was on the other?

QUESTION 8
Can you name the female singer who once sang with Soul II Soul and scored her own top twenty hit in 1990 with 'Livin' in the Light'?

QUESTION 9
Fairground Attraction topped the chart in 1988 with 'Perfect', and their follow-up also made the top ten in the same year. What was the title?

QUESTION 10
Can you name the group that achieved a top twenty hit in 1999 with a hit called 'The Kids Aren't Alright' that was featured in the movie *The Faculty* the same year?

Q1
Adele

Q2
'Little Donkey'

Q3
'Hurt'

Q4
Katie Melua

Q5
'All out of Love'

Q6
Slash from Guns N' Roses

Q7
Patrick Juvet

Q8
The KLF

Q9
Girls! Girls! Girls!

Q10
The Zutons

QUIZ 039 POPMASTER

QUESTION 1
Which successful boy band scored a top five hit in 1996 with 'Coming Home Now'?

QUESTION 2
Apart from singer and actor David Soul's two number one hits, 'Don't Give Up on Us' and 'Silver Lady', can you name either of his other two top ten hits?

QUESTION 3
Can you name the comedy actor who reached the top forty in 2001 with 'Are You Lookin' at Me'?

QUESTION 4
Which female singer recorded a 1985 top five cover version of Michael Jackson's hit from 1972 called 'Ben'?

QUESTION 5
The Drifters scored debut hits in the Sixties with songs that both included the word 'Dance' in the title – one was 'Save the Last Dance for Me', but what was the title of their first chart entry?

QUESTION 6
Can you name the group that achieved their first top ten hit in 1993 with 'Too Young to Die'?

QUESTION 7
What was the name of the Australian singer who reached the top ten in 2008 with 'Black and Gold'?

QUESTION 8
According to his 1983 top three hit, which Guyanan-born performer was walking down 'Electric Avenue'?

QUESTION 9
Can you name the band whose album Are You Experienced made the top ten in 1967?

QUESTION 10
Which duo made the top three in 1997 with the theme tune to the movie *The Saint*?

POPMASTER QUIZ 040

QUESTION 1
Which 1954 Johnnie Ray number one did Elvis Presley successfully revive in 1964?

QUESTION 2
Can you name the female singer who achieved a top ten hit in 2007 with 'No One'?

QUESTION 3
In 1991, Scritti Politti – with more than a little help from Shabba Ranks – made the top twenty with which Lennon and McCartney song?

QUESTION 4
Released in 1980, what was the title of the only top forty hit by American singer Stacy Lattisaw?

QUESTION 5
Can you name the group whose single 'All I Need is a Miracle' was first released in 1986 but failed to make the top forty until re-issued and re-mixed in 1996?

QUESTION 6
The duo Hudson-Ford had two top twenty hits in the Seventies. The first was 'Pick Up the Pieces' – what was the title of the second?

QUESTION 7
Which group's first top ten hit came in 1996 with 'Stupid Girl', which contained a sample of 'Train in Vain' by The Clash?

QUESTION 8
Which legendary guitarist and singer had a number one album in 1994 called From the Cradle?

QUESTION 9
In 2008, Leona Lewis achieved a number two hit with a double 'A'-sided release. One of the songs was 'Better in Time', but what was the title of the religious-themed ballad on the other side?

QUESTION 10
Name the singer who made his top 40 debut in 1960 with 'Lucky Devil' – more than two years before he scored his first number one.

Q1
Johnny Mathis

Q2
MN8

Q3
EMF

Q4
XTC

Q5
Olivia Newton-John

Q6
Clock

Q7
'Dreams of Children'

Q8
Caron Wheeler

Q9
'Find My Love'

Q10
The Offspring

QUIZ 041 POPMASTER

Q1
Boyzone

Q2
'Going in with My Eyes Open',
'Let's Have a Quiet Night In'

Q3
Ricky Tomlinson

Q4
Marti Webb

Q5
'Dance with Me'

Q6
Jamiroquai

Q7
Sam Sparro

Q8
Eddy Grant

Q9
The Jimi Hendrix Experience

Q10
Orbital

QUESTION 1
From which successful movie did the 1994 top ten hit single 'All for Love', by Bryan Adams, Rod Stewart and Sting, come?

QUESTION 2
In 1980, The Tourists scored a top ten hit with 'So Good to be Back Home', but which more successful act did they evolve into?

QUESTION 3
Can you name the top ten hit from 1967 by Herman's Hermits that was successfully revived in 1976 by the Carpenters?

QUESTION 4
Which 1997 number one hit by Eternal featured vocals by Bebe Winans?

QUESTION 5
What is the song title shared by a top three hit by Racey in 1979, a top ten hit by Ultimate Kaos in 1994 and a number two hit by Rachel Stevens, also from 2004?

QUESTION 6
In the Eighties, Wham! achieved four consecutive top ten hits with their first four releases. Can you name the first?

QUESTION 7
According to his 1975 top twenty hit, which singer-songwriter claimed 'I Don't Love You but I Think I Like You'?

QUESTION 8
From 1985, what was the title of the top twenty hit recorded by Lisa Lisa and Cult Jam with Full Force?

QUESTION 9
Can you name the rock band that topped the albums chart in 1971 with Fireball?

QUESTION 10
What was the title of the official song of the England World Cup football squad from 2002 that became a top ten hit for Ant & Dec?

POPMASTER QUIZ 042

QUESTION 1
In 1974, Johnny Bristol achieved his only hit as a performer with 'Hang on in There Baby' – the same year he wrote the only number one for The Osmonds. What was the title?

QUESTION 2
Procol Harum topped the chart in 1967 with 'A Whiter Shade of Pale' and their follow-up became their only other top ten hit. Can you remember the title?

QUESTION 3
What is the song title shared by Anita Ward's 1979 number one hit and the 1991 top twenty hit by Monie Love vs Adeva?

QUESTION 4
Can you name the female group that achieved a top ten hit in 2001 with 'All Hooked Up'?

QUESTION 5
Which group made their top forty debut in 2001 with a song called 'Red'?

QUESTION 6
The late Bobby Darin achieved two number one hits in 1959 – the first was 'Dream Lover', what was the second?

QUESTION 7
McFly scored a number one in 2007 with their double 'A'-sided hit 'Baby's Coming Back'. What was the other song on the release?

QUESTION 8
Which family group's only number one album was their 1986 release Silk and Steel?

QUESTION 9
Can you name the female singer who achieved a top ten hit in 2003 with 'Mixed Up World'?

QUESTION 10
Fine Young Cannibals achieved a number of hits in the Eighties, but only one of their records made the top twenty in the Nineties. Can you name it?

QUIZ 043 POPMASTER

Q1
The Three Musketeers

Q2
Eurythmics

Q3
'There's a Kind of Hush'

Q4
'I Wanna be the Only One'

Q5
'Some Girls'

Q6
'Young Guns (Go for It)'

Q7
Gilbert O'Sullivan

Q8
'I Wonder if I Take You Home'

Q9
Deep Purple

Q10
'We're on the Ball'

QUESTION 1
Which 1978 top twenty hit by Billy Joel did Barry White take back into the chart towards the end of the same year?

QUESTION 2
What was the title of Marty Wilde's 1961 top ten hit that was an even bigger hit in the same year for the original American version by Bobby Vee?

QUESTION 3
'Doo Wop (That Thing)' was the first solo top ten hit by Lauryn Hill, who had previously been a member of two successful groups. Can you name either of them?

QUESTION 4
Can you name the group that topped the albums chart in 1993 with Walthamstow?

QUESTION 5
In 1961, two versions of the title theme to the movie *Pepe* made the top twenty. The bigger hit was by Duane Eddy, but who recorded the other version?

QUESTION 6
In 1990, Twenty 4 Seven featuring Captain Hollywood achieved two top twenty hits – the second was 'Are You Dreaming', but what was the title of the first?

QUESTION 7
In 1981, which group reached the top ten for the first time in nearly six years with 'We'll Bring the House Down'?

QUESTION 8
Can you name the rapper who topped the chart in 2000 with his single 'Stan'?

QUESTION 9
The title track of Lemar's second album was a top ten single for the singer in 2005 – what was it called?

QUESTION 10
Can you name the singer-songwriter who had his only top forty hit in 1979 with 'Just When I Needed You Most'?

POPMASTER QUIZ 044

QUESTION 1
The American R&B group Raydio achieved two top forty hits in the Seventies – the first was 'Jack and Jill', but can you name the second?

QUESTION 2
What was the title of Bitty McLean's 1994 top ten hit that had originally been a hit in 1967 for The Mamas and The Papas?

QUESTION 3
Which successful group made their final appearance in the top ten with 'Big Apple'?

QUESTION 4
In 1979, which Jamaican singer made the top twenty for the first and only time in his career with 'Money in My Pocket'?

QUESTION 5
From the year 2000, can you name the French group who topped the UK chart with 'Lady (Hear Me Tonight)'?

QUESTION 6
Can you name the singer-songwriter who topped the albums chart in 1987 with ...Nothing Like the Sun?

QUESTION 7
In 1979, which soul group made their final appearance in the top forty with 'Sing a Happy Song'?

QUESTION 8
What hit song title is shared by Billy Fury in 1961, Pet Shop Boys in 1991 and Will Young in 2011?

QUESTION 9
Which rock band had a top ten hit in 1995 with 'This Ain't a Love Song'?

QUESTION 10
As a duo, what was the collective name with which David Grant and Peter "Sketch" Martin scored their only top ten hit with 'Intuition' in 1981?

QUIZ 045 POPMASTER

Q1
'Just the Way You Are'

Q2
'Rubber Ball'

Q3
Fugees, Refugee All Stars

Q4
East 17

Q5
Russ Conway

Q6
'I Can't Stand It'

Q7
Slade

Q8
Eminem

Q9
'Time to Grow'

Q10
Randy Vanwarmer

QUESTION 1
Which group's only top ten hit came in 1970 with a revival of The Animals' 1964 number one 'The House of the Rising Sun'?

QUESTION 2
Can you name the Irish female singer who had top five hits in the Fifties with 'Softly, Softly',' 'Let Me Go Lover' and 'Evermore'?

QUESTION 3
Harold Melvin & The Blue Notes scored two top ten hits in the Seventies. The first was 'If You Don't Know Me by Now', but what was the title of the second?

QUESTION 4
In 1993, which group achieved a top three hit with 'Exterminate!' that was featured in the movie *Batman Returns*?

QUESTION 5
Can you name the band that topped the albums chart in 2015 with How Big, How Blue, How Beautiful?

QUESTION 6
Under what name did Linda Green and Herbert Feemster record their 1979 top five hit 'Reunited'?

QUESTION 7
'It's Your Day Today' became the last of 11 top forty entries for this singer in the Sixties. Can you name him?

QUESTION 8
Which female singer topped the singles chart for two weeks in 2009 with 'Fight for this Love'?

QUESTION 9
From 1978, what was the title of the only top twenty hit by Blue Öyster Cult?

QUESTION 10
Which hit song made the top forty in 1978 for Rose Royce, Jimmy Nail in 1985 and Double Trouble featuring Janette Sewell and Carl Brown in 1990?

POPMASTER QUIZ 046

QUESTION 1
Anthony Newley achieved two number one hits in 1960. The first was called 'Why', but what was the title of the second?

QUESTION 2
Can you name the vocal trio who topped the chart in 2004 with 'Baby Cakes'?

QUESTION 3
Released at the end of 1979, what is the title of the top three hit duet by Billy Preston and Syreeta that was featured in the movie *Fastbreak*?

QUESTION 4
Which group had a top twenty hit in the early Seventies with the song 'Come Softly to Me' that had previously been a top ten hit for both The Fleetwoods and Frankie Vaughan and The Kaye Sisters in 1959?

QUESTION 5
Can you name the act that topped the albums chart in 2015 with Wilder Mind?

QUESTION 6
From 1978, what was the title of the only top twenty hit achieved by Australian singer John Paul Young?

QUESTION 7
Which legendary pop star released the single 'Golden' in 2015 in celebration of his 75th birthday?

QUESTION 8
Can you name the female singer who made the top ten in 2004 with 'Don't Tell Me' and 'My Happy Ending'?

QUESTION 9
What was the title of the 1973 top twenty hit by New York City that The Pasadenas took into the top five in 1992?

QUESTION 10
Which 1964 top twenty hit by Elvis Presley did ZZ Top take all the way into the top ten in 1992?

Q1
'Is this a Love Thing'

Q2
'Dedicated to the One I Love'

Q3
Kajagoogoo

Q4
Dennis Brown

Q5
Modjo

Q6
Sting

Q7
The O'Jays

Q8
'Jealousy'

Q9
Bon Jovi

Q10
Linx

QUIZ 047 POPMASTER

Q1
Frijid Pink

Q2
Ruby Murray

Q3
'Don't Leave Me this Way'

Q4
Snap! (featuring Niki Haris)

Q5
Florence + The Machine

Q6
Peaches and Herb

Q7
P.J. Proby

Q8
Cheryl Cole

Q9
'(Don't Fear) the Reaper'

Q10
'Love Don't Live Here Anymore'

QUESTION 1
In 1966, which female singer achieved her eighth consecutive top forty hit with 'Nothing Comes Easy'?

QUESTION 2
From 1980, what was the title of the only number one hit achieved by American R&B group Odyssey?

QUESTION 3
Which American singer-songwriter achieved his only top ten hit in 1978 with 'Lucky Star'?

QUESTION 4
Can you name the group that achieved two top twenty hits in the Nineties with 'Sixty Mile Smile' and 'Beautiful Day'?

QUESTION 5
What was the title of the 1987 top three hit by Mental as Anything that was featured in the movie *Crocodile Dundee*?

QUESTION 6
Which Canadian singer was featured on Chris Brown's 2011 top twenty hit 'Next to You'?

QUESTION 7
Over the years, whose group, The Bluesbreakers, has included Eric Clapton, Peter Green and Mick Taylor in its line-up?

QUESTION 8
The Bee Gees achieved two number one hits in the Sixties – 'Massachusetts' was the first one, what was the other?

QUESTION 9
Can you name the band that topped the albums chart in 2002 with Heathen Chemistry?

QUESTION 10
What was the title of the 1979 chart hit by Patrick Hernandez, the one-time backing singer for Madonna?

POPMASTER QUIZ 048

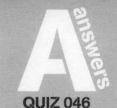

QUESTION 1
In 1970, the soul act The Chairmen of the Board scored two top ten hits – the first was 'Give Me Just a Little More Time', but what was the title of the second?

Q1
'Do You Mind'

QUESTION 2
Can you name the group that achieved their first top twenty hit in 1982 with 'Promised You a Miracle'?

Q2
3 of a Kind

QUESTION 3
In 1972, Andy Williams released a song with the subtitle '(Speak Softly Love)' that was the love theme from which classic movie?

Q3
'With You I'm Born Again'

QUESTION 4
What is the name of the actress who has been a cast regular in *Coronation Street* since the Eighties (playing Audrey Roberts) who had a top ten hit in 1968 with 'Where Will You Be'?

Q4
The New Seekers

QUESTION 5
Can you name the rock band that topped the albums chart in 2011 with Wasting Light?

Q5
Mumford & Sons

QUESTION 6
What was the title of the 1995 top twenty hit by Jimmy Somerville that had previously been a 1975 top five hit for Susan Cadogan?

Q6
'Love is in the Air'

QUESTION 7
Which group released their single 'Lucky You' in 1994 but didn't see it make the top forty until its re-issue the following year?

Q7
Cliff Richard

QUESTION 8
Can you name the French duo that made their chart debut in 1998 with 'Sexy Boy'?

Q8
Avril Lavigne

QUESTION 9
Released in 1963, what was the title of the only number one hit achieved by The Dave Clark Five, at the start of 1964?

Q9
'I'm Doin' Fine Now' (spelt 'Doing' on the Pasadenas version)

QUESTION 10
Which legendary female singer topped both the American and UK charts in 1980 with the Barry and Robin Gibb song 'Woman in Love'?

Q10
'Viva Las Vegas'

QUIZ 049 POPMASTER

Q1
Sandie Shaw

Q2
'Use it Up and Wear it Out'

Q3
Dean Friedman

Q4
3 Colours Red

Q5
'Live it Up'

Q6
Justin Bieber

Q7
John Mayall

Q8
'I've Gotta Get a Message to You'

Q9
Oasis

Q10
'Born to be Alive'

QUESTION 1
Which group reached the top five in 1967 with their hit single 'Zabadak!'?

QUESTION 2
In 1978, Glasgow-born Frankie Miller achieved his only UK top ten hit. What was the title?

QUESTION 3
Can you name the pianist and orchestra leader whose only hit made the top five in 1963 with the theme from the movie *The Legion's Last Patrol*?

QUESTION 4
Which rock performer's top ten album, released in 1983, was called Midnight at the Lost and Found?

QUESTION 5
Can you name the Lionel Bart musical which featured Harry Secombe's 1963 top twenty hit 'If I Ruled the World'?

QUESTION 6
What was the title of the 1991 top ten duet by Kylie Minogue and Keith Washington?

QUESTION 7
Can you name the *X Factor* winner who had the 2010 Christmas number one with 'When We Collide'?

QUESTION 8
As featured in the Seventies TV series *Rock Follies*, what was the only chart hit for its stars – Julie Covington, Rula Lenska, Charlotte Cornwell and Sue Jones-Davies?

QUESTION 9
Which group ended a run of five consecutive top ten hits in the Nineties with 'Sun Hits the Sky'?

QUESTION 10
First released in the Sixties, which Tamla Motown single by The Elgins failed to chart until it was re-issued in 1971, making the top three?

POPMASTER QUIZ 050

QUESTION 1
According to their 1979 hit album and single, which group were enjoying 'Breakfast in America'?

QUESTION 2
What was the title of Junior's 1982 chart debut and only solo top ten hit?

QUESTION 3
Which country and western singer topped the chart for 11 weeks in 1955 with 'Rose Marie'?

QUESTION 4
In 1972, David Cassidy achieved his first solo hit – a double 'A' side that peaked at number two. One of the songs was 'Could it be Forever' – what was the other?

QUESTION 5
In the year 2000, Coldplay had their first top twenty hit. What was the title?

QUESTION 6
Between 1996 and 1997, Alisha's Attic had three consecutive hits that all peaked at number 12 in the chart. Can you name one of these hits?

QUESTION 7
What was the name of the group that reached the top ten in 1980 with the revival of the 1958 number two hit 'Tom Hark', by Elias and His Zigzag Jive Flutes?

QUESTION 8
Despite their popularity, folk duo Peter, Paul and Mary only achieved one top ten hit. What was it called?

QUESTION 9
Can you remember the name of the German studio group that topped the singles chart in 2000 with 'Toca's Miracle'?

QUESTION 10
In 1978, which legendary rock band had a top three album called And Then There Were Three?

QUIZ 049

Dave Dee, Dozy, Beaky, Mick & Tich

Q2
'Darlin''

Q3
Ken Thorne

Q4
Meat Loaf

Q5
Pickwick

Q6
'If You Were with Me Now'

Q7
Matt Cardle

Q8
'OK?'

Q9
Supergrass

Q10
'Heaven Must Have Sent You'

54

QUIZ 051 POPMASTER

QUESTION 1
Can you name the Jamaican reggae star who achieved a top twenty hit in 1967 with 'Al Capone'?

QUESTION 2
Which of these Rod Stewart records remained at the top of the chart the longest: 'Baby Jane', 'Da Ya Think I'm Sexy?' or 'Sailing'?

QUESTION 3
American soul singer Donna Allen released two top ten hits in the Eighties. One was 'Joy and Pain', but what was the title of the other?

QUESTION 4
Which female singer topped the chart in 2006 with 'Smile', and in 2009 with 'The Fear'?

QUESTION 5
Can you name the group whose third hit in a run of five top five singles in the early Eighties was 'Say Hello, Wave Goodbye'?

QUESTION 6
Tom Jones enjoyed a top five hit in 1988 that featured Art of Noise and a song called 'Kiss', but do you know who wrote it?

QUESTION 7
Can you name the group that made their 1990 top twenty chart debut with 'Loaded'?

QUESTION 8
What was the title of the only solo top forty hit recorded by David Ruffin following his departure from The Temptations?

QUESTION 9
On which 1975 album by Wings did their hit single 'Listen to What the Man Said' first appear?

QUESTION 10
Can you name the legendary soul singer who in 1966 took 'Land of a Thousand Dances' into the top forty?

POPMASTER QUIZ 052

QUESTION 1
Who topped the chart in 1953 for two weeks with 'Hey Joe'?

QUESTION 2
Can you name the female singer who was featured on Quincy Jones's 1981 top twenty hit 'Razzamatazz'?

QUESTION 3
Which American group made the top ten in 1997 with a cover of The Ohio Players' US number one 'Love Rollercoaster'?

QUESTION 4
Which of these Donny Osmond hits remained at number one for the most weeks: 'Puppy Love', 'The Twelfth of Never' or 'Young Love'?

QUESTION 5
Which 1965 number one hit by The Rolling Stones featured the Jagger and Richards song 'Play with Fire' on the 'B' side?

QUESTION 6
Can you name the American singer-songwriter whose only top twenty hit was his 1976 cover of Unit 4 + 2's 1965 number one 'Concrete and Clay'?

QUESTION 7
Which UK number one by the Spice Girls was their only record to top the American chart?

QUESTION 8
In 1991, George Michael made the top forty with 'Heal the Pain' that he re-recorded for his 2006 greatest hits album. Can you remember who sang with him on the new version?

QUESTION 9
Which 'sensational' band made the top ten of the albums chart in 1975 with Tomorrow Belongs to Me?

QUESTION 10
American singer Debbie Gibson achieved two top ten hits in the Eighties. One was 'Shake Your Love', but what was the other called?

Q1
Supertramp

Q2
'Mama Used to Say'

Q3
Slim Whitman

Q4
'Cherish'

Q5
'Yellow'

Q6
'Alisha Rules the World', 'Indestructible', 'Air We Breathe'

Q7
The Piranhas

Q8
'Leaving on a Jet Plane'

Q9
Fragma

Q10
Genesis

55

QUIZ 053 POPMASTER

Q1
Prince Buster

Q2
'Sailing' (4 weeks)

Q3
'Serious'

Q4
Lily Allen

Q5
Soft Cell

Q6
Prince

Q7
Primal Scream

Q8
'Walk Away from Love'

Q9
Venus and Mars

Q10
Wilson Pickett

QUESTION 1
Which band topped the chart for two weeks in 1983 with 'Is There Something I Should Know'?

QUESTION 2
Can you name the female singer who made her top forty chart debut in 1992 with 'Feel So High'?

QUESTION 3
In 1974, Donny and Marie Osmond reached number two with their first hit duet, 'I'm Leaving It (All) Up to You'. It was a revival of a 1963 American number one by which other duo?

QUESTION 4
Which of these Shakin' Stevens hits remained at the top of the singles chart the longest: 'Green Door', 'This Ole House' or 'Merry Christmas Everyone'?

QUESTION 5
Which 1965 number one hit by The Beatles featured the Lennon and McCartney song 'I'm Down' on the 'B' side?

QUESTION 6
Can you name the act that successfully revived Roger Miller's 1965 number one 'King of the Road' on their 1990 top ten EP with that title?

QUESTION 7
Which American female singer made the top three of the albums chart in 1989 with The Other Side of the Mirror?

QUESTION 8
After a number of minor hits, which band finally made the top twenty in 2004 with 'The Bucket'?

QUESTION 9
In 1993, House of Pain achieved their only UK top ten hit with a double 'A'-sided hit. One of the songs was called 'Top o' the Morning to Ya' – what was the other?

QUESTION 10
Which two singers achieved a top ten duet in 1992 with the theme song to the musical Beauty and the Beast?

POPMASTER QUIZ 054

QUESTION 1
In 1969, which group had a hit with '(Call Me) Number One' – but only made it to number two?

QUESTION 2
According to their 2006 top ten hit, which successful duo claimed 'I'm with Stupid'?

QUESTION 3
Can you name the singer who achieved a number one album in 1984 with 'Human's Lib'?

QUESTION 4
Which 1978 top ten hit by Third World was successfully covered in 1991 by Heavy D & The Boys?

QUESTION 5
According to their 1983 top twenty hit, which legendary band invited us to 'Come Dancing'?

QUESTION 6
Can you name the American singer who, in 2004, achieved her 11th consecutive UK top forty hit with 'Welcome to My Truth'?

QUESTION 7
In 1993, which band made their chart debut when they reached number two with 'The Key the Secret'?

QUESTION 8
As a solo performer, Midge Ure scored two top ten hits in the Eighties. The second of these was his number one 'If I Was', but what was the title of the first?

QUESTION 9
Which of these Madonna hits remained at the top of the chart the longest: 'Into the Groove', 'Papa Don't Preach' or 'Like a Prayer'?

QUESTION 10
Can you name the Beatles album on which their song 'Carry that Weight' first appeared?

Q1
Frankie Laine

Q2
Patti Austin

Q3
Red Hot Chili Peppers

Q4
'Puppy Love' (5 weeks)

Q5
'The Last Time'

Q6
Randy Edelman

Q7
'Wannabe'

Q8
Paul McCartney

Q9
The Sensational Alex Harvey Band

Q10
'Foolish Beat'

QUIZ 055 POPMASTER

Q1
Duran Duran

Q2
Des'ree

Q3
Dale & Grace

Q4
'Green Door' (4 weeks)

Q5
'Help!'

Q6
The Proclaimers

Q7
Stevie Nicks

Q8
Kings of Leon

Q9
'Jump Around'

Q10
Celine Dion & Peabo Bryson

QUESTION 1
In 1961, which American female singer reached the top five with the title song to the movie in which she starred, *Where the Boys Are*?

QUESTION 2
Can you name the actor who reached number two in the singles chart in 1978 with 'Sandy'?

QUESTION 3
Which Salvation Army pop group achieved a top forty hit in 1964 with 'It's an Open Secret'?

QUESTION 4
Featured in the Eighties movie *Footloose*, which female singer found herself 'Holding out for a Hero'?

QUESTION 5
Which of these hits by Slade remained at the top of the chart the longest: 'Mama Weer All Crazee Now', Skweeze Me Pleeze Me' or 'Coz I Luv You'?

QUESTION 6
Can you name the female Jamaican singer who in 1994 made the top three with 'You Don't Love Me (No No No)' but never managed to repeat her success?

QUESTION 7
Which 2003 top five hit by P!nk featured William Orbit and could be heard in the movie *Charlie's Angels: Full Throttle*?

QUESTION 8
Can you name the group that topped the albums chart in 1980 with Flesh and Blood?

QUESTION 9
In 2002, which successful male vocalist joined Jakatta on his top ten hit 'My Vision'?

QUESTION 10
American rapper Robert Van Winkle scored two big UK hits when 'Ice Ice Baby' topped the chart and 'Play that Funky Music' made the top ten. Under what name did he release the records?

POPMASTER QUIZ 056

QUESTION 1
Which American female singer graced the top twenty for the final time in 1988 with 'Radio Romance'?

QUESTION 2
Part of a run of seven consecutive top twenty hits during the Eighties, who considered himself a 'Wide Boy'?

QUESTION 3
In 1991, which legendary group made the top ten for the first time in just over eight years with 'No Son of Mine'?

QUESTION 4
Two versions of the song 'Answer Me' topped the chart in 1953 – one was by Frankie Laine, but who recorded the other?

QUESTION 5
Under what collective name did the UK pop-folk act that comprised of Luke Concannon and John Parker achieve their 2005 number one with 'JCB Song'?

QUESTION 6
Can you name the Brazilian musician who reached the top ten in 1973 with his jazz version of 'Also Sprach Zarathustra (2001)' but never made the chart again?

QUESTION 7
In 1985, which female singer topped the albums chart for two weeks with Promise?

QUESTION 8
Who, according to his 1990 top ten hit, checked in at the 'Blue Hotel'?

QUESTION 9
Which of these David Bowie hits remained at number one the longest: 'Space Oddity', 'Let's Dance' or 'Ashes to Ashes'?

QUESTION 10
In 1994, which American group reached number two with 'Baby I Love Your Way' but never bothered the top forty again?

Q1
The Tremeloes

Q2
Pet Shop Boys

Q3
Howard Jones

Q4
'Now that We've Found Love'

Q5
The Kinks

Q6
Anastacia

Q7
Urban Cookie Collective

Q8
'No Regrets'

Q9
'Into the Groove' (4 weeks)

Q10
Abbey Road

QUIZ 057 POPMASTER

Q1
Connie Francis

Q2
John Travolta

Q3
The Joy Strings

Q4
Bonnie Tyler

Q5
'Coz I Luv You' (4 weeks)

Q6
Dawn Penn

Q7
'Feel Good Time'

Q8
Roxy Music

Q9
Seal

Q10
Vanilla Ice

QUESTION 1
From 1973, what was the title of Clifford T Ward's only top 40 hit?

QUESTION 2
On which album did Heart's 1987 American number one and UK top three hit 'Alone' first appear?

QUESTION 3
Ricky Ross, who achieved his only solo top forty hit in 1996 with 'Radio On', was once a member of which successful band?

QUESTION 4
Can you name the instrumental outfit that topped the chart in 1958 for three weeks with 'Hoots Mon'?

QUESTION 5
Which of these Elvis Presley hits spent the longest time at number one: 'The Wonder of You', 'Way Down' or 'Crying in the Chapel'?

QUESTION 6
What hit song title is shared by a 1994 top forty hit by Killing Joke and a 1994 number one by Robbie Williams?

QUESTION 7
Richard Melville Hall made the top ten in 1997 with 'James Bond Theme', featured in the movie *Tomorrow Never Dies*. Under what name did he release the hit?

QUESTION 8
From 1967, what was the title of the only top forty hit achieved by Simon Dupree & The Big Sound?

QUESTION 9
Can you name the UK rock band that achieved number one albums in the Seventies with 'Houses of the Holy, The Song Remains the Same and In Through the Out Door?

QUESTION 10
Which Canadian group topped the American chart and made the UK top five in 1999 with 'One Week'?

POPMASTER QUIZ 058

QUESTION 1
On which Moody Blues album did their 1970 number two hit 'Question' first appear as the opening track?

QUESTION 2
A 1960 top three hit by Elvis Presley has the same title as a 1984 top twenty hit by Lionel Richie and Trevor Walters' top ten cover of Richie's song that same year. What is that shared song title?

QUESTION 3
The lead singer of which successful rock band achieved solo top ten hits in 1997 with 'Midnight in Chelsea' and 'Queen of New Orleans'?

QUESTION 4
Can you name the group whose hits between 1970 and 1973 included 'Good Morning Freedom', 'The Banner Man' and 'Randy'?

QUESTION 5
In 1992, which group topped the chart for four weeks with 'Ebeneezer Goode'?

QUESTION 6
Which American vocalist reached number two on the albums chart in 1979 with Fate for Breakfast?

QUESTION 7
What was the name of the American singer who topped the singles chart in early 1959 with 'The Day the Rains Came'?

QUESTION 8
In 1983, JoBoxers achieved two consecutive top ten hits. The first was 'Boxer Beat', but what was the second?

QUESTION 9
X Factor winner Joe McElderry topped the chart for just one week with his debut single – his only number one to date. Can you name it?

QUESTION 10
Which of these Cliff Richard hits remained at number one for the longest period of time: 'Congratulations', 'Summer Holiday' or 'The Young Ones'?

Q1
Tiffany

Q2
Nik Kershaw

Q3
Genesis

Q4
David Whitfield

Q5
Nizlopi

Q6
Deodato

Q7
Sade

Q8
Chris Isaak

Q9
'Let's Dance' (3 weeks)

Q10
Big Mountain

QUIZ 059 POPMASTER

Q1
'Gaye'

QUESTION 1
With which successful group of the Sixties and Seventies was Junior Campbell once a member?

Q2
Bad Animals

QUESTION 2
Can you name the Jamaican singer who achieved his one and only top forty hit in the mid-Seventies with a cover of The Allman Brothers song 'Midnight Rider'?

Q3
Deacon Blue

QUESTION 3
The disco band Shalamar achieved four top ten hits in the Eighties: 'I Can Make You Feel Good', 'A Night to Remember', 'There it Is' and which other single?

Q4
Lord Rockingham's XI

QUESTION 4
Which of these hits by The Police spent the most weeks at number one on the UK singles chart: 'Message in a Bottle', 'Walking on the Moon' or 'Don't Stand So Close to Me'?

Q5
'The Wonder of You' (6 weeks)

QUESTION 5
Can you name the American duo that topped the chart for five weeks in 1958 with 'When'?

Q6
'Millennium'

QUESTION 6
By what name is British singer Dominique Atkins, who achieved a top ten hit in 1995 with 'Not Over Yet', better known?

Q7
Moby

QUESTION 7
Can you name the American group whose only top ten album was their 1977 release Aja?

Q8
'Kites'

QUESTION 8
Which Irish rock band achieved top twenty hits in the Nineties with 'Linger', 'Salvation' and 'Promises'?

Q9
Led Zeppelin

QUESTION 9
What song title is shared by a top twenty hit from 1966 by The Mindbenders, a number one from 1980 by David Bowie and a top twenty from 1997 by Faith No More?

Q10
Barenaked Ladies

QUESTION 10
Can you name the group who took Grandmaster Flash and Melle Mel's 1983 top ten hit 'White Lines (Don't Don't do It)' back into the top twenty in 1995, minus one of the 'Don't's?

POPMASTER QUIZ 060

QUESTION 1
Can you name the 1967 number one album by The Monkees on which their chart-topping single 'I'm a Believer' was the closing track?

QUESTION 2
Which one-time member of the Spice Girls topped the chart in 2000 with 'I Turn to You'?

QUESTION 3
What song title is shared by a 1962 top twenty hit by Nat 'King' Cole and George Shearing, a top ten hit from 1991 by Simple Minds and a number two hit from 2005 by Oasis?

QUESTION 4
Which 1969 Marvin Gaye top five hit featured the song 'Wherever I Lay My Hat' on the 'B' side?

QUESTION 5
In 2005, the Kaiser Chiefs re-issued their debut top forty hit 'I Predict a Riot' with which song to make it a double 'A' side?

QUESTION 6
Which group had top ten albums in the Seventies with Sheet Music, The Original Soundtrack and Deceptive Bends?

QUESTION 7
Which famous orchestra leader and composer wrote the theme tune to the successful Sixties movie and cartoon series *The Pink Panther*?

QUESTION 8
Can you name the group that made their 1980 top twenty chart debut with 'Messages'?

QUESTION 9
'I Should Coco' was a 1995 number one album for which successful band?

QUESTION 10
Which of these Michael Jackson hits spent the most weeks at number one: 'One Day in Your Life', 'Earth Song' or 'I Just Can't Stop Loving You'?

Q1
A Question of Balance

Q2
'Stuck on You'

Q3
Jon Bon Jovi

Q4
Blue Mink

Q5
The Shamen

Q6
Art Garfunkel

Q7
Jane Morgan

Q8
'Just Got Lucky'

Q9
'The Climb'

Q10
'The Young Ones' (6 weeks)

QUIZ 061 POPMASTER

A BITE OF THE APPLE

These are questions about artists that were signed or had records released on The Beatles' Apple label

Q1
Marmalade

Q2
Paul Davidson

Q3
'Dead Giveaway'

Q4
'Don't Stand So Close to Me'
(4 weeks)

Q5
The Kalin Twins

Q6
Grace

Q7
Steely Dan

Q8
The Cranberries

Q9
'Ashes to Ashes'

Q10
Duran Duran

QUESTION 1
What was the title of the only solo hit single release on the Apple label by Billy Preston?

QUESTION 2
Which female singer had top ten hits on Apple with 'Goodbye' and 'Temma Harbour'?

QUESTION 3
Can you name the singer and songwriter who released his debut eponymous album, produced by Peter Asher, on the Apple label in 1968?

QUESTION 4
Which member of The Beatles achieved an American number one and a UK top ten hit in 1973 with 'Give Me Love (Give Me Peace on Earth)'?

QUESTION 5
From 1971, what was the title of Paul McCartney's first solo hit on the Apple label?

QUESTION 6
What was the name of the group that scored two top forty hits on Apple, 'Hare Krishna Mantra' in 1969 and 'Govinda' the following year?

QUESTION 7
Although not a hit, which member of The Ronettes released just one single on Apple in 1971 - the George Harrison composition 'Try Some, Buy Some'?

QUESTION 8
Can you name the group who achieved their one and only top 40 hit in 1969 with a medley of 'Golden Slumbers' and 'Carry that Weight'?

QUESTION 9
Featuring Paul McCartney on 'kazoo' and Harry Nilsson on backing vocals, which member of The Beatles made the top five in 1974 with the revival of Johnny Burnette's 1961 hit 'You're Sixteen'?

QUESTION 10
Which group achieved three top ten hits on Apple in the early Seventies - 'Come and Get It', 'No Matter What' and 'Day After Day'?

POPMASTER QUIZ 062
ALTERNATIVE ARTISTS

QUESTION 1
Members of Duran Duran released a Top 10 single called 'Election Day' in 1985, but under what name did they record this hit?

QUESTION 2
...Other members of Duran Duran teamed up with singer Robert Palmer and Chic drummer Tony Thompson as The Power Station to record a Top 20 debut single produced by Bernard Edwards of Chic. What was it called?

QUESTION 3
Under what name did Siouxsie Sioux and Budgie of Siouxsie & The Banshees have hits with the songs 'Right Now' and 'Miss the Girl'?

QUESTION 4
Electronic, Monaco and The Other Two have all been alternative chart acts by members of which group?

QUESTION 5
Which two members of Talking Heads began the group Tom Tom Club in 1981?

QUESTION 6
Name all five of the musicians who, alongside successful individual careers, came together to form The Traveling Wilburys.

QUESTION 7
David Bowie put his solo career to one side in the late Eighties to form a band with Reeves Gabrels and brothers Hunt and Tony Sales. What were they called?

QUESTION 8
Sir John Johns, The Red Curtain, Lord Cornelius Plum and E.I.E.I. Owen were the 'members' of The Dukes of Stratosphear – a pseudonym used by which British band?

QUESTION 9
Alex Turner of The Last Shadow Puppets is also lead singer with a band whose five studio albums to date have all reached number one. What is that group?

QUESTION 10
When Motörhead teamed up with Girlschool to record the 1981 Top 5 EP 'St Valentine's Day Massacre', they were jointly known by what name?

Q1
More of The Monkees

Q2
Melanie C

Q3
'Let there be Love'

Q4
'Too Busy Thinking 'bout My Baby'

Q5
'Sink that Ship'

Q6
10cc

Q7
Henry Mancini

Q8
Orchestral Manoeuvres in the Dark

Q9
Supergrass

Q10
'Earth Song' (6 weeks)

ALTERNATIVE VERSIONS

Q1
'That's the Way God Planned It'

Q2
Mary Hopkin

Q3
James Taylor

Q4
George Harrison

Q5
'Another Day'

Q6
The Radha Krishna Temple

Q7
Ronnie Spector

Q8
Trash

Q9
Ringo Starr

Q10
Badfinger

QUESTION 1
Tracey Ullman's 1984 hit 'My Guy' was her gender-reversed version of the song 'My Girl', which was a hit in 1980 for which group?

QUESTION 2
Following the success of The Simon Park Orchestra's 1973 number one 'Eye Level', Matt Monro had a Top 40 hit with a vocal version of that tune. What was it called?

QUESTION 3
Name both the groups that have reached number one with versions of the song 'The Tide is High'.

QUESTION 4
Having co-written and produced the song 'China Girl' for Iggy Pop's 1977 album The Idiot, David Bowie decided to record his own version of the song for which 1983 number one album?

QUESTION 5
Having reached No.69 for just one week in 1994 with the song 'Missing', which duo reached the Top 3 in 1995, spent 22 weeks on the chart and over a year on the American chart with a remixed version of that same song?

QUESTION 6
In the same week in September 1978, The Jacksons and a singer called Mick Jackson both entered the Top 40 with their versions of which song?

QUESTION 7
'Do They Know it's Christmas?' has been number one for Band Aid, Band Aid II, Band Aid 20 and Band Aid 30, but who sings the opening line on each of the versions?

QUESTION 8
In 1993, Barry Manilow had a Top 40 hit with a dance version of a song that had been a Top 30 hit for him in the late Seventies. What is the song?

QUESTION 9
'He was Beautiful' was a 1979 Top 20 vocal version of the theme from The Deer Hunter. It was recorded by Iris who?

QUESTION 10
Ron and Russell Mael of Sparks featured in the video of a cover version of their song 'This Town Ain't Big Enough for Both of Us', a 2005 Top 10 hit for Justin Hawkins of The Darkness recording under what name?

POPMASTER QUIZ 064
ANAGRAMOPHONES (1)

Unpick the names of these chart artists and their number one singles; the year is given as a clue. Anagrams do not include definite or indefinite articles.

QUESTION 1
"Icier Hellhole Loin" (1984)

QUESTION 2
"Masquerade in Hype on Hob" (1975)

QUESTION 3
"Bewailing Crass Pen" (1996)

QUESTION 4
"Bracketed Toilet Ties" (1965)

QUESTION 5
"Exorbitant Spies Cry" (2004)

QUESTION 6
"Naive Bicycle Ace Alibi" (1990)

QUESTION 7
"Beanbag and Quince" (1976)

QUESTION 8
"Dim Clamps Bled Filthiness" (1989)

QUESTION 9
"Flared Yoga Package" (2009)

QUESTION 10
"Do Be Soothsaying Vicar Bob" (1966)

QUIZ 062
ALTERNATIVE ARTISTS

Q1
Arcadia

Q2
'Some Like it Hot'

Q3
The Creatures

Q4
New Order

Q5
Tina Weymouth and Chris Frantz

Q6
Bob Dylan, George Harrison, Jeff Lynne, Roy Orbison, Tom Petty

Q7
Tin Machine

Q8
XTC

Q9
Arctic Monkeys

Q10
Headgirl

Q1
Madness

Q2
'And You Smiled'

Q3
Blondie, Atomic Kitten

Q4
Let's Dance

Q5
Everything but the Girl

Q6
'Blame it on the Boogie' (Mick Jackson was one of the song's co-writers)

Q7
Paul Young, Kylie Minogue, Chris Martin (Coldplay), One Direction

Q8
'Could it be Magic'

Q9
Iris Williams

Q10
British Whale

QUIZ 065 POPMASTER

ANAGRAMOPHONES (2)

Unpick the names of these chart artists and their number one singles; the year is given as a clue. Anagrams do not include definite or indefinite articles.

QUESTION 1
"Wasted Migratory Game" (1971)

QUESTION 2
"Despairingly for Drum" (1995)

QUESTION 3
"Hot Pest Bows Depressingly" (1986)

QUESTION 4
"We Involuntarily Howl Egg" (2003)

QUESTION 5
"Nosh Toll on Networking Monkeys" (1969)

QUESTION 6
"Adaptable Nuts Rule" (1983)

QUESTION 7
"Barnstorm Warp Tattoo" (1978)

QUESTION 8
"Beer Vehicle" (1998)

QUESTION 9
"Cry Milk Leakage" (2007)

QUESTION 10
"Incompatible Eagles Toes" (1979)

POPMASTER QUIZ 066

ANAGRAMOPHONES (3)

Unpick the names of these chart artists and their number one singles. The year is given as a clue. Anagrams do not include definite or indefinite articles.

QUESTION 1
"Carefree Mania" (1982)

QUESTION 2
"Ably Compose Bonanza" (1996)

QUESTION 3
"Uneasy Weedily Honoree" (1977)

QUESTION 4
"Alien Yells Mill" (2006)

QUESTION 5
"Drab Matrimony Numbers" (1965)

QUESTION 6
"Extreme Malt Rags" (1972)

QUESTION 7
"Garnishes Eden" (2014)

QUESTION 8
"Forget Lamp Damn Infantrymen" (1966)

QUESTION 9
"Goodbye Loftier Whole Workstations" (1984)

QUESTION 10
"Yellowing Identical Hormone" (1998)

QUIZ 064
ANAGRAMOPHONES (1)

Q1
Lionel Richie, 'Hello'

Q2
Queen, 'Bohemian Rhapsody'

Q3
Spice Girls, 'Wannabe'

Q4
Beatles, 'Ticket to Ride'

Q5
Britney Spears, 'Toxic'

Q6
Vanilla Ice, 'Ice Ice Baby'

Q7
ABBA, 'Dancing Queen'

Q8
Simple Minds, 'Belfast Child'

Q9
Lady Gaga, 'Poker Face'

Q10
Beach Boys, 'Good Vibrations'

QUIZ 067 POPMASTER
AND YOUR BIRD CAN SING

QUIZ 065
ANAGRAMOPHONES (2)

Q1
Rod Stewart, 'Maggie May'

Q2
Simply Red, 'Fairground'

Q3
Pet Shop Boys, 'West End Girls'

Q4
Will Young, 'Leave Right Now'

Q5
Rolling Stones, 'Honky Tonk Women'

Q6
Spandau Ballet, 'True'

Q7
Boomtown Rats, 'Rat Trap'

Q8
Cher, 'Believe'

Q9
Mika, 'Grace Kelly'

Q10
Police, 'Message in a Bottle'

QUESTION 1
Which album by the Eagles includes the songs 'New Kid in Town', 'Life in the Fast Lane' and 'The Last Resort'?

QUESTION 2
The songs 'There Goes the Fear' and 'Black and White Town' were Top 10 hits in the Noughties for which group?

QUESTION 3
Which song has been a hit for both Inez & Charlie Foxx in 1969 and Carly Simon and James Taylor in 1974?

QUESTION 4
Who had her debut Top 40 hit in 1992 with the Top 5 song 'All I Wanna Do'?

QUESTION 5
Which of our feathered friends features in the title of a 1982 Top 10 hit by Kid Creole & The Coconuts?

QUESTION 6
Children from the Abbey Hey Junior School had a Top 20 hit in 1979 with 'The Sparrow', which they recorded under what name?

QUESTION 7
Lemon Jelly reached the Top 20 in 2003 with the track 'Nice Weather for...' what?

QUESTION 8
Gerry Rafferty sang about a 'Night Owl' on his 1979 solo hit, but with which group did he have three Top 40 hits earlier that decade?

QUESTION 9
The song 'L'Oiseau et L'Enfant' won the 1977 Eurovision Song Contest. It was sung by Marie Myriam, but did she win for Belgium, France, Luxembourg or Switzerland?

QUESTION 10
The theme song to the children's TV programme *Magpie* was recorded by The Murgatroyd Band – a pseudonym for members of which Sixties hit group?

POPMASTER QUIZ 068
BALL AND CHAIN

QUIZ 066
ANAGRAMOPHONES (3)

QUESTION 1
In 1960, which American singer achieved his first UK top ten hit with 'Chain Gang'?

QUESTION 2
Which group scored a 1982 top twenty hit in the UK with 'Back on the Chain Gang', which was featured in the movie *King of Comedy*?

QUESTION 3
Which musical featured the 1989 UK number two hit for Michael Ball, 'Love Changes Everything'?

QUESTION 4
Which vocal group successfully revived Diana Ross's 1986 number one hit, 'Chain Reaction', in 2001?

QUESTION 5
Can you name the female pianist who successfully recorded a medley of old standards that made the UK top five in 1957 under the title 'Let's Have a Ball'?

QUESTION 6
Which duo made the top twenty in 1988 with 'Chains of Love'?

QUESTION 7
Released in 1970, which Motown group achieved their third UK top ten hit with 'Ball of Confusion'?

QUESTION 8
Can you name the well-known trumpeter who achieved a number of hits with his jazz band including 'Midnight in Moscow', 'March of the Siamese Children' and 'The Green Leaves of Summer'?

QUESTION 9
In 1990, which successful reggae band from Birmingham made the top forty with their single 'Wear You to the Ball'?

QUESTION 10
What was the title of the 1972 debut top ten hit for Roy Wood's group, Wizzard?

QUIZ 066
ANAGRAMOPHONES (3)

Q1
Irene Cara, 'Fame'

Q2
Babylon Zoo, 'Spaceman'

Q3
Leo Sayer, 'When I Need You'

Q4
Lily Allen, 'Smile'

Q5
Byrds, 'Mr Tambourine Man'

Q6
T.Rex, 'Telegram Sam'

Q7
Ed Sheeran, 'Sing'

Q8
Manfred Mann, 'Pretty Flamingo'

Q9
Frankie Goes to Hollywood, 'Two Tribes'

Q10
Celine Dion, 'My Heart Will Go On'

71

Q1
Hotel California

Q2
Doves

Q3
'Mockingbird'

Q4
Sheryl Crow

Q5
Pigeon ('Stool Pigeon' reached number 7 in the summer of '82)

Q6
The Ramblers

Q7
Ducks

Q8
Stealers Wheel

Q9
France

Q10
The Spencer Davis Group

QUIZ 069 POPMASTER
BEAT THE INTRO (1)

Can you name the hit single from the artist, year and description of how the song starts?

QUESTION 1
Kraftwerk – 1975 – a lorry or large vehicle starting up and pulling away

QUESTION 2
Kate Bush – 1989 – the sound of peeling church bells

QUESTION 3
Take That – 1995 – the 'Tuba Mirum' trumpet fanfare from Verdi's 'Requiem'

QUESTION 4
Madonna featuring Justin Timberlake – 2008 – the brief ticking of a watch or clock

QUESTION 5
Duran Duran – 1981 – the sound of a fast motor drive of a camera

QUESTION 6
Jonathan Richman – 1977 – counting up to 6

QUESTION 7
Michael Jackson – 1983 – a creaky door or coffin lid opening and some footsteps

QUESTION 8
A-ha – 1990 – a muffled thunder storm

QUESTION 9
Bobby Goldsboro – 1973 – the sound of waves on a beach

QUESTION 10
Mika – 2007 – a satisfied slurping through a straw

POPMASTER QUIZ 070

BEAT THE INTRO (2)

Can you name the hit single from the artist, year and description of how the song starts?

QUESTION 1
The Sweet – 1974 – a crowd chanting "We Want Sweet"

QUESTION 2
George Michael – 1987 – the introduction to an old Wham! song played on an organ

QUESTION 3
Madonna – 2005 – a ticking clock or watch (again, very brief!)

QUESTION 4
Blondie – 1978 – the sound of a phone ringing in the earpiece

QUESTION 5
Malcolm McLaren – 1983 – the sound of a skipping rope

QUESTION 6
Electric Light Orchestra – 1978 – a weather report on the radio

QUESTION 7
The Monkees – 1967 – the studio saying that the 'take' is 7A

QUESTION 8
The Specials – 1981 – the sound of howling wind

QUESTION 9
Roxy Music – 1975 – the sound of someone walking along and opening a car door

QUESTION 10
Lady Gaga – 2009 – a solo violin playing with the sound of wind and the sea in the background

QUIZ 071 POPMASTER
BELL RINGERS

Q1
'Autobahn'

Q2
'The Sensual World'

Q3
'Never Forget'

Q4
'4 Minutes'

Q5
'Girls on Film'

Q6
'Roadrunner'

Q7
'Thriller'

Q8
'Crying in the Rain'

Q9
'Summer (The First Time)'

Q10
'Big Girl (You Are Beautiful)'

QUESTION 1
Showaddywaddy's final Bell release became their only number one, previously an American hit in the Sixties for Curtis Lee. What was the title?

QUESTION 2
Can you name the female American group who achieved their only top twenty hit in 1968 with a song called 'Captain of Your Ship'?

QUESTION 3
The Bell label had quite a reputation for creating one-off hits, such was the case with a UK studio group named Mardi Gras who covered a 1969 top five Marvin Gaye hit in 1972. Can you name it?

QUESTION 4
In 1973, David Cassidy achieved his second and final number one with a double 'A'-sided hit. One song was 'The Puppy Song', but what was the other?

QUESTION 5
What was the name of the made-up group that scored a major hit in 1971 with 'Johnny Reggae'?

QUESTION 6
The all-girl group from Philadelphia, First Choice, achieved two top twenty hits on Bell in 1973. The first was 'Armed and Extremely Dangerous', what was the second?

QUESTION 7
Also in 1973, Barry Blue achieved two top ten hits on Bell - the first was 'Dancin' (On a Saturday Night)', what was the other?

QUESTION 8
Can you name the first hit for The Box Tops from 1967 that topped the American chart for four weeks?

QUESTION 9
After his 1962 hit 'Hey Baby', American singer Bruce Channel had to wait over six years before he next made the chart, with his only hit on Bell. What was the title?

QUESTION 10
From 1975, what was the title of the Bay City Rollers' first number one - a revival of a 1965 song by The Four Seasons?

POPMASTER QUIZ 072

BIG STARS LITTLE HITS (1)

Can you name these famous artists or bands from the titles of three of their smaller Top 40 hits?

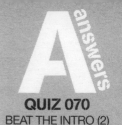

QUESTION 1
'New Amsterdam' in 1980, 'Veronica' in 1989, 'Sulky Girl' in 1994

QUESTION 2
'Sunny' in 1966, 'Dark Lady' in 1974, 'Not Enough Love in the World' in 1996

QUESTION 3
'Missionary Man' in 1987, 'Angel' in 1990, '17 Again' in 2000

QUESTION 4
'Rock 'n' Roll Damnation' in 1978, 'Shake Your Foundations' in 1986, 'Hard as a Rock' in 1995

QUESTION 5
'Thinking of You' in 2009, 'The One that Got Away' in 2011, 'Birthday' in 2014

QUESTION 6
'Blowin' in the Wind' in 1966, 'We Can Work it Out' in 1971, 'That Girl' in 1982

QUESTION 7
'Living in Sin' in 1989, 'Misunderstood' in 2002, 'Because We Can' in 2013

QUESTION 8
'Sign of the Times' in 1978, 'The Right Stuff' in 1987, 'Will You Love Me Tomorrow' in 1993

QUESTION 9
'Wild Honey' in 1967, 'Rock and Roll Music' in 1976, 'Here Comes the Night' in 1979

QUESTION 10
'Treat Her Like a Lady' in 1999, 'Goodbye's (The Saddest Word)' in 2002, 'Loved Me Back to Life' in 2013

QUIZ 070
BEAT THE INTRO (2)

Q1
'Teenage Rampage'

Q2
'Faith' (organ is playing a slow version of Wham!'s Freedom)

Q3
'Hung Up'

Q4
'Hanging on the Telephone'

Q5
'Double Dutch'

Q6
'Mr Blue Sky'

Q7
'Daydream Believer'

Q8
'Ghost Town'

Q9
'Love is the Drug'

Q10
'Alejandro'

QUIZ 073 POPMASTER

BIG STARS LITTLE HITS (2)

Can you name these famous artists or bands from the titles of three of their smaller Top 40 hits?

Q1
'Under the Moon of Love'

Q2
Reparata & The Delrons

Q3
'Too Busy Thinking 'bout My Baby'

Q4
'Daydreamer'

Q5
The Piglets

Q6
'Smarty Pants'

Q7
'Do You Wanna Dance?'

Q8
'The Letter'

Q9
'Keep On'

Q10
'Bye Bye Baby'

QUESTION 1
'Wow' in 1979, 'The Big Sky' in 1986, 'Moments of Pleasure' in 1993

QUESTION 2
'Love in Itself' in 1983, 'Policy of Truth' in 1990, 'Wrong' in 2009

QUESTION 3
'Heaven' in 1985, 'Do I Have to Say the Words?' in 1992, 'Flying' in 2004

QUESTION 4
'Loving You is Sweeter than Ever' in 1966, 'Just Seven Numbers (Can Straighten out My Life)' in 1971, 'Don't Walk Away' in 1981

QUESTION 5
'Modern Girl' in 1984, 'Runnin' for the Red Light (I Gotta Life)' in 1996, 'Couldn't Have Said it Better' in 2003

QUESTION 6
'Popscene' in 1992, 'MOR' in 1997, 'Good Song' in 2003

QUESTION 7
'Movin' Out (Anthony's Song)' in 1978, 'The Longest Time' in 1984, 'All About Soul' in 1993

QUESTION 8
'Careless Memories' in 1981, 'Meet El Presidente' in 1987, 'Electric Barbarella' in 1999

QUESTION 9
'(Ain't That) Just Like Me' in 1963, 'King Midas in Reverse' in 1967, 'Long Cool Woman in a Black Dress' in 1972

QUESTION 10
'Shapes that Go Together' in 1994, 'Summer Moved On' in 2000, 'Cosy Prisons' in 2006

POPMASTER QUIZ 074

BIG STARS LITTLE HITS (3)

Can you name these famous artists or bands from the titles of three of their smaller Top 40 hits?

QUESTION 1
'Love Loves to Love Love' in 1967, 'Take Your Mama for a Ride' in 1975, 'Where the Poor Boys Dance' in 2000

QUESTION 2
'La Tristesse Durera (Scream to a Sigh)' in 1993, 'Let Robeson Sing' in 2001, '(It's Not War) Just the End of Love' in 2010

QUESTION 3
'Get Down and Get with It' in 1971, 'My Baby Left Me - That's All Right' in 1977, 'All Join Hands' in 1984

QUESTION 4
'Being Boring' in 1990, 'I Get Along' in 2002, 'It Doesn't Often Snow at Christmas' in 2009

QUESTION 5
'Thieves Like Us' in 1984, 'Spooky' in 1993, 'Waiting for the Sirens' Call' in 2005

QUESTION 6
'Think' in 1968, 'Angel' in 1973, 'A Rose is Still a Rose' in 1998

QUESTION 7
'You Could Have Been a Lady' in 1971, 'Are You Getting Enough of What Makes You Happy' in 1980, 'Tears on the Telephone' in 1983

QUESTION 8
'Word is Out' in 1991, 'Some Kind of Bliss' in 1997, 'Timebomb' in 2012

QUESTION 9
'America' in 1974, 'Imperial Wizard' in 1979, 'Falling Angels Riding' in 1985

QUESTION 10
'Infidelity' in 1987, 'Thrill Me' in 1992, 'Fake' in 2003

Q1
Elvis Costello

Q2
Cher

Q3
Eurythmics

Q4
AC/DC

Q5
Katy Perry

Q6
Stevie Wonder

Q7
Bon Jovi

Q8
Bryan Ferry

Q9
The Beach Boys

Q10
Celine Dion

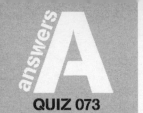

QUIZ 075 POPMASTER
BOY BANDS

QUESTION 1
Which 1996 number one by Take That was a cover of a Bee Gees song?

QUESTION 2
Which member of The Jonas Brothers had a Top 3 solo single in 2015 with 'Jealous'?

QUESTION 3
Which Christmas carol formed part of a Christmas double 'A' side Top 3 single by Bros in 1988?

QUESTION 4
Lee, Jimmy and Spike had a run of 13 hit singles in the Nineties, recorded under what name?

QUESTION 5
Which 1974 single by the Bay City Rollers was also the title of their 1975 TV series?

QUESTION 6
Which boy band had Top 10 hits in 2014 with the songs 'Tonight (We Live Forever)' and 'You Got it All'?

QUESTION 7
What was the title of the 1983 number one by New Edition?

QUESTION 8
The songs 'Anything', 'Why' and 'I Need You' were Top 10 hits for Michael Jackson's nephews Taj, Taryll and TJ in the mid-Nineties. What was the name of this trio?

QUESTION 9
A1 reached number one in 2000 with their version of which A-ha song?

QUESTION 10
'You Just Might See Me Cry' was the title of a Top 3 hit in 1976 for Our Kid, who found success having appeared on which TV talent show?

POPMASTER QUIZ 076

CARTOON HEROES
Questions about animated and puppet pop stars

QUESTION 1
Which two puppet pigs released their first single in 1958 and just failed to reach the Top 40 in 1993 with their version of Jackie Wilson's 'Reet Petite'?

QUESTION 2
Which character, a fixture of Saturday TV in the early '90s, knocked Take That's 'Babe' off number one to have the Christmas number one in 1993 with an eponymously titled single?

QUESTION 3
Which favourite seasonal song scraped the bottom of the Top 40 as a cover version for Keith Harris and Orville the duck at Christmas in 1985?

QUESTION 4
Roland Rat Superstar had two Top 40 hits in the Eighties. Name either of them.

QUESTION 5
What was the name of Kermit the Frog's nephew who sang the Top 10 Muppet hit 'Halfway Down the Stairs' in 1977?

QUESTION 6
The Smurfs' entire singles chart career in the Top 40 has been in just two years – three hits in 1978 and two in 1996. 'The Smurf Song' was the 1978 Top 3 debut. Name one of the other four songs.

QUESTION 7
Under what name did American rap duo James Alpem and Richard Usher record their 1990 number one 'Turtle Power'?

QUESTION 8
Who was the voice of Chef from *South Park*, who reached number one in 1999 with 'Chocolate Salty Balls (PS I Love You)'?

QUESTION 9
Only one of The Wombles' Top 10 singles did not include a derivation of the furry creatures' name in the title – what was it called?

QUESTION 10
Although they never had a UK hit single, what was the name of Hanna-Barbera's early Seventies cartoon about an all-girl mystery-solving pop group?

Answers

QUIZ 074
BIG STARS LITTLE HITS (3)

Q1
Lulu

Q2
Manic Street Preachers

Q3
Slade

Q4
Pet Shop Boys

Q5
New Order

Q6
Aretha Franklin

Q7
Hot Chocolate

Q8
Kylie Minogue

Q9
David Essex

Q10
Simply Red

QUIZ 075
BOY BANDS

CHRISTMAS LIST

This round is about hit Christmas songs that made the UK top forty between 1955 and 2003

Q1
'How Deep is Your Love'

QUESTION 1
Can you name the singer who achieved a number one hit in 1985 with 'Merry Christmas Everyone' and a top forty hit in 1991 with 'I'll be Home this Christmas'?

Q2
Nick Jonas

QUESTION 2
Which legendary singer-songwriter found himself in the top ten in 1985 with his version of 'Santa Claus is Coming to Town'?

Q3
'Silent Night' (double 'A' side with 'Cat Among the Pigeons')

QUESTION 3
In 1973, which group, featuring vocal backing by The Suedettes plus The Stockland Green Bilateral School First Year Choir with additional noises by Miss Snob and Class 3C, were in the top five with 'I Wish it Could be Christmas Everyday'?

Q4
911

QUESTION 4
Can you name the crooner who topped the singles chart in 1955 for three weeks with 'Christmas Alphabet' and made the top ten in 1956 with 'Christmas Island'?

Q5
'Shang-a-Lang'

QUESTION 5
Which rock band scored a number two hit in 2003 with 'Christmas Time (Don't Let the Bells End)'?

Q6
Union J

QUESTION 6
What was the title of Greg Lake's 1975 solo Christmas number two hit?

Q7
'Candy Girl'

QUESTION 7
Can you name the Cuban female singer who made the top ten in 1992 with 'Christmas Through Your Eyes'?

Q8
3T

QUESTION 8
Although never a major hit, which Chris Rea Yuletide song has gained steady sales since its initial release in 1988?

Q9
'Take on Me'

QUESTION 9
Which successful glam-rock band topped the chart in 1974 for four weeks with 'Lonely this Christmas'?

Q10
New Faces

QUESTION 10
Which classic 1962 Brenda Lee hit was successfully revived by Mel Smith and Kim Wilde in 1987?

POPMASTER QUIZ 078

CLASSIC POP

These are hit singles with a link to classical music

QUESTION 1
Eric Carmen's only UK hit – later covered by Celine Dion – contains a portion of Rachmaninoff's 'Piano Concerto No.2'. What is it called?

QUESTION 2
The Farm's 'Altogether Now', Coolio's 'C U When U Get There' and 'Welcome to the Black Parade' by My Chemical Romance are all said to have been inspired by a canon written by which 17th-century German composer?

QUESTION 3
The melody of the late 19th-century song ''O Sole Mio' was used for which Elvis Presley number one?

QUESTION 4
Tchaikovsky's '1812 Overture' is referenced in the riff and bassline of the 1967 debut hit by The Move. What is the song called?

QUESTION 5
David Shire's 'Night on Disco Mountain', from *Saturday Night Fever*, is his take on 'Night on Bald Mountain' by which composer?

QUESTION 6
In 1984, Malcolm McLaren had a Top 20 hit with song subtitled '(Un Bel di Vedremo)' – the name of the aria by Puccini which features in the single. What was it called?

QUESTION 7
'Jupiter, the Bringer of Jollity', from Holst's Planets suites, is used as the basis of the melody for which 1973 hit by Manfred Mann's Earth Band?

QUESTION 8
The guitar riff in the 2001 Muse hit 'Plug in Baby' has often been compared to part of 'Toccata and Fugue in D minor' by which Baroque composer?

QUESTION 9
Mozart's 'Symphony No.41' features in which of The Wombles' hit singles?

QUESTION 10
Which 2001 single by Janet Jackson includes a small section of one of Erik Satie's 'Gymnopédies'?

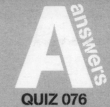
QUIZ 076
CARTOON HEROES

Q1
Pinky & Perky

Q2
Mr Blobby

Q3
'White Christmas'

Q4
'Rat Rapping', 'Love Me Tender'

Q5
Robin

Q6 *Dippety Day', 'Christmas in Smurfland' (both '78), 'I've Got a Little Puppy', 'Your Christmas Wish' (both '96)*

Q7
Partners in Kryme

Q8
Isaac Hayes

Q9
'Banana Rock'

Q10
Josie & The Pussycats

Q1
Shakin' Stevens

Q2
Bruce Springsteen

Q3
Wizzard

Q4
Dickie Valentine

Q5
The Darkness

Q6
'I Believe in Father Christmas'

Q7
Gloria Estefan

Q8
'Driving Home for Christmas'

Q9
Mud

Q10
'Rockin' Around the Christmas Tree'

QUIZ 079 POPMASTER
CONNECTIONS (1)

In each case, what is the common link between these three bands, songs or artists?

QUESTION 1
Madness, Bananarama, Gorillaz

QUESTION 2
'Someday' by The Gap Band, 'I Feel for You' by Chaka Khan, 'There Must be an Angel (Playing with My Heart)' by Eurythmics

QUESTION 3
Martin Fry of ABC, Shaun Ryder of Happy Mondays, Phil Oakey of Human League

QUESTION 4
'Miss Sarajevo' by Passengers, 'True' by Spandau Ballet, 'Where Do You Go to (My Lovely)' by Peter Sarstedt

QUESTION 5
'Street Life' by The Crusaders, 'Killer' by Adamski, 'In a Broken Dream' by Python Lee Jackson

QUESTION 6
New Order's 'True Faith', The Police's 'Synchronicity II', Bastille's 'Pompeii'

QUESTION 7
ABBA's 'Does Your Mother Know', Oasis' 'Don't Look Back in Anger', Eagles' 'Take it to the Limit'

QUESTION 8
The chart acts Wah, Wham & Yell

QUESTION 9
'Walking in the Rain with the One I Love' by Love Unlimited, 'Heartache' by Pepsi & Shirley, 'Central Park Arrest' by Thunderthighs

QUESTION 10
'My Way' by Frank Sinatra, 'Amoureuse' by Kiki Dee, 'Seasons in the Sun' by Terry Jacks

POPMASTER QUIZ 080

CONNECTIONS (2)

In each case, what is the common link between these three bands, songs or artists?

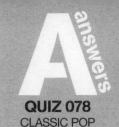

QUESTION 1
Madness, U2, The Police

QUESTION 2
Dave Edmunds' 'Girls Talk', Lulu's 'The Man Who Sold the World', Sinead O'Connor's 'Nothing Compares 2 U'

QUESTION 3
Cher, Denise Marsa, Sheena Easton

QUESTION 4
Shayne Ward, Sarah Harding of Girls Aloud, Davy Jones of The Monkees

QUESTION 5
'Unchained Melody', 'Bohemian Rhapsody', 'The Ballad of John and Yoko'

QUESTION 6
Ace, Squeeze, Mike & The Mechanics

QUESTION 7
Living in a Box, Talk Talk, Jilted John

QUESTION 8
Kim Carnes, Suzanne Vega, Elton John

QUESTION 9
Beats International, Freakpower, The Housemartins

QUESTION 10
Eurythmics, The Police, Sheena Easton

QUIZ 078
CLASSIC POP

Q1
'All by Myself'

Q2
Johann Pachelbel

Q3
'It's Now or Never'

Q4
'Night of Fear'

Q5
Modest Mussorgsky

Q6
'Madam Butterfly'

Q7
'Joybringer'

Q8
J.S. Bach

Q9
'Minuetto Allegretto'

Q10
'Someone to Call My Lover'

QUIZ 079
CONNECTIONS (1)

Q1 *All recorded songs with actors in the title ('Michael Caine', 'Robert De Niro's Waiting', 'Clint Eastwood')*

Q2
All feature Stevie Wonder harmonica solos

Q3 *Have all name-checked themselves in their own songs ('The Look of Love', 'Hallelujah', 'Love Action')*

Q4 *Songs name-checking other acts in the lyrics (East 17, Marvin Gaye, The Rolling Stones/Sacha Distel)*

Q5 *There is no credit for the lead singer on each of the singles (Randy Crawford, Seal, Rod Stewart)*

Q6
Titles of songs not in the lyrics

Q7 *Singer on all three hits isn't the group's usual lead singer(s) (Björn Ulvaeus, Noel Gallagher, Randy Meisner)*

Q8 *All have exclamation marks after the band name (left off the question so as not to give it away!)*

Q9 *Debut hits for backing vocalists recording in their own right (Barry White, Wham!, various)*

Q10
All three songs originally had French lyrics

QUIZ 081 POPMASTER
DAYS OF THE WEEK

QUESTION 1
Topping the UK chart for three weeks in 1979, what was the title of Blondie's second number one hit?

QUESTION 2
Which group achieved a UK top five hit in the year 2000 with 'Sunday Morning Call', taken from their album Standing on the Shoulder of Giants?

QUESTION 3
From 1966, can you name the first UK top ten hit and American number one for The Mamas and The Papas?

QUESTION 4
Can you name the group who in 1992 achieved their first UK top twenty hit in nearly six years with 'Tuesday Morning'?

QUESTION 5
With which group did Feargal Sharkey enjoy the 1980 UK top twenty hit 'Wednesday Week'?

QUESTION 6
Originally written for the computer game Omikron: The Nomad Soul, who had a top twenty hit with the song 'Thursday's Child', taken from his 1999 album Hours?

QUESTION 7
Can you name the singer and blues guitarist who scored a top forty hit in 1987 with the revival of The Easybeats' 1966 top ten chart entry 'Friday on My Mind'?

QUESTION 8
In 2006, which boy band achieved a UK top three hit with their double 'A'-sided single 'Sorry's Not Good Enough' and 'Friday Night'?

QUESTION 9
What hit song title is shared by Whigfield in 1994, Suede in 1997 and UD Project in 2004?

QUESTION 10
Released at the end of 1985, which soul singer joined Cherrelle on 'Saturday Love', her UK top ten hit in early 1986?

POPMASTER QUIZ 082
FEELING CRAZY

QUESTION 1
Which Welsh classical singer turned pop star enjoyed a top three hit in 2005 with 'Crazy Chick'?

QUESTION 2
Can you name the rock band that made the UK top five in 1987 with 'Crazy Crazy Nights'?

QUESTION 3
What was the title of the debut hit and number one from The Temperance Seven in 1961?

QUESTION 4
Can you name the American female singer who achieved her biggest UK hit in 1989 with 'Miss You Like Crazy'?

QUESTION 5
In 1979, which legendary rock band topped the American chart for four weeks and reached number two in the UK with 'Crazy Little Thing Called Love'?

QUESTION 6
What is the common song title shared on hits by Patsy Cline, Mud, Gnarls Barkley and Seal, to name but four?

QUESTION 7
Two hit songs by Madonna were featured in the 1985 movie *Vision Quest*, in which she played a club singer. One was 'Gambler' – what was the other?

QUESTION 8
In 1981, which singer achieved his second top ten hit with the song 'You Drive Me Crazy'?

QUESTION 9
Which American family group earned their first UK top three hit in 1972 with 'Crazy Horses'?

QUESTION 10
Can you name the female singer who made her 2003 UK chart debut with 'The Closest Thing to Crazy'?

Q1
Lead singers are all known by single names (Suggs, Bono, Sting)

Q2 Hit covers of songs not released as UK singles by the song's writers (Elvis Costello, David Bowie, Prince)

Q3 Uncredited female voices on hit duets ('Dead Ringer for Love', 'Lucky Stars', 'U Got the Look')

Q4
Have all acted in Coronation Street

Q5
Number one songs whose title isn't in the lyrics

Q6
Paul Carrack has played in all three groups

Q7
Have all had hits with eponymously titled songs

Q8 All recorded songs about actresses ('Bette Davis Eyes', 'Marlene on the Wall', 'Candle in the Wind')

Q9
All featured Norman Cook before he recorded as Fatboy Slim

Q10 Their second Top 40 hit was a re-release, previously having been a Top 75 hit before their Top 40 debut!

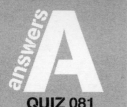

QUIZ 083 POPMASTER
FEET

QUIZ 081
DAYS OF THE WEEK

Q1
'Sunday Girl'

Q2
Oasis

Q3
'Monday Monday'

Q4
The Pogues

Q5
The Undertones

Q6
David Bowie

Q7
Gary Moore

Q8
McFly

Q9
'Saturday Night'

Q10
Alexander O'Neal

QUESTION 1
Which group followed their 1967 number one hit 'Baby Now that I've Found You' with 'Back on My Feet Again'?

QUESTION 2
The song 'Head over Feet' became the first UK top ten hit for which Canadian female singer in 1996?

QUESTION 3
Can you name the singer who released a 2015 single, 'Fire Under My Feet', from her first album in nearly two years, I Am?

QUESTION 4
Who sang the title song to the 1984 movie and had a top ten hit with the song 'Footloose'?

QUESTION 5
Which child actor turned singing star had a 1952 top three UK hit with 'Feet Up! (Pat Her on the Po-Po)'?

QUESTION 6
In 1974, what was the title of the first number one hit for glam-rock band Mud?

QUESTION 7
What was the title of the song that gave both Steve Lawrence and Ronnie Carroll a hit in 1960 and was successfully revived in 1981 by Showaddywaddy?

QUESTION 8
What was the title of the hit single by rock band Embrace that became the official song of the England World Cup Squad during their 2006 FIFA World Cup campaign?

QUESTION 9
Can you name the instrumental group that topped the UK singles chart in 1963 with 'Foot Tapper'?

QUESTION 10
What was the collective name of the Danish duo consisting of Jesper Mortensen and Jeppe Laursen who achieved a UK top three hit in 2003 with 'Move Your Feet'?

POPMASTER QUIZ 084

FESTIVAL FEVER

QUESTION 1
Who reached number one in 1970 with the song 'Woodstock'?

QUESTION 2
...and which singer-songwriter and guitarist was the opening act at that 1969 festival?

QUESTION 3
Which band had to pull out of a headlining slot at the 2015 Glastonbury festival due to the drummer breaking his leg?

QUESTION 4
Founded in 1971, in which country is the Roskilde Festival held?

QUESTION 5
The songs 'Ooh Stick You!', 'Ugly' and 'School's Out' were all hits in 2000 for a female duo who were bottled off the main stage at Reading Festival after just two songs in that same year. Name the duo.

QUESTION 6
Having been revived in 2002, which festival takes place at Seaclose Park?

QUESTION 7
Lilith Fair was a concert tour and travelling music festival of the late Nineties founded by which Canadian singer and songwriter?

QUESTION 8
Who was brought on stage in a wheelchair at the 1992 Reading Festival?

QUESTION 9
Which UK festival is held in both Hylands Park, Chelmsford, and Weston Park, Staffordshire?

QUESTION 10
Which American festival was founded in the early Nineties by Perry Farrell of Jane's Addiction?

QUIZ 085 POPMASTER
FILM MUSIC (1)

Q1
The Foundations

Q2
Alanis Morissette

Q3
Leona Lewis

Q4
Kenny Loggins

Q5
Guy Mitchell

Q6
'Tiger Feet'

Q7
'Footsteps'

Q8
'World at Your Feet'

Q9
The Shadows

Q10
Junior Senior

QUESTION 1
'The Power of Love' by Huey Lewis & The News features in which Michael J. Fox film of the mid-Eighties?

QUESTION 2
What is the title of Seal's hit song that appears over the closing credits of the film *Batman Forever*?

QUESTION 3
What was the title of the 1995 number one by Coolio featuring LV that featured in the film *Dangerous Minds*, starring Michelle Pfeiffer?

QUESTION 4
For what film did the Pet Shop Boys write the Dusty Springfield hit 'Nothing has Been Proved'?

QUESTION 5
Which American singer has acted in the films *The Social Network, Friends with Benefits and Trouble with the Curve*?

QUESTION 6
Name one of the three original hit singles from the soundtrack to the 1988 film *Buster*.

QUESTION 7
Purple Rain was the title of Prince's first film. What was his second, released in 1986?

QUESTION 8
'(Best That You Can Do)' is the subtitle to the theme song from a film starring Dudley Moore that became the only UK Top 40 hit for Christopher Cross – what is the full title of the song?

QUESTION 9
Released in America in 1960, what was the name of the first film Elvis Presley made after he left the army?

QUESTION 10
The song 'Raindrops Keep Falling on My Head', made famous by both BJ Thomas and Sacha Distel, featured in which 1969 film?

POPMASTER QUIZ 086

FILM MUSIC (2)

QUESTION 1
Who appeared in the films *The Hunger, Merry Christmas, Mr Lawrence* and *Absolute Beginners* in the Eighties?

QUESTION 2
Which group sang 'Disco Inferno' on the *Saturday Night Fever* soundtrack?

QUESTION 3
Released in 1996, what is the title of Celine Dion's UK Top 5 and US No.1 single subtitled '(Theme from *Up Close and Personal*)?

QUESTION 4
In which 1970 film did Mick Jagger star as the lead character in a story about a 19th-century Australian bushranger?

QUESTION 5
What was the title of Lionel Richie's hit song from the film *White Nights*, starring Mikhail Baryshnikov and Gregory Hines?

QUESTION 6
Who recorded the soundtrack to the film *When Harry Met Sally* and starred himself in the films *Memphis Belle, Copycat* and *Little Man Tate*?

QUESTION 7
Duran Duran got their name from a character in which fantasy film starring Jane Fonda?

QUESTION 8
In which film did Eminem appear as the character Jimmy "B-Rabbit" Smith Jr?

QUESTION 9
Actor Will Smith's 2002 Top 3 hit 'Black Suits Comin (Nod Ya Head)' featured vocals from Tra-Knox and was featured on the soundtrack to which of his hit movies?

QUESTION 10
Which American singer won a 'Best Supporting Actress' Academy award for her role in the film *Dreamgirls*?

Q1
Matthews' Southern Comfort

Q2
Richie Havens

Q3
Foo Fighters

Q4
Denmark

Q5
Daphne & Celeste

Q6
Isle of Wight Festival

Q7
Sarah McLachlan

Q8
Kurt Cobain of Nirvana

Q9
V Festival

Q10
Lollapalooza

QUIZ 087 POPMASTER
GUEST STARRING (1)
Guest appearances by chart artists on other hit records

Q1
Back to the Future

Q2
'Kiss from a Rose'

Q3
'Gangsta's Paradise'

Q4
Scandal

Q5
Justin Timberlake

Q6 *'A Groovy Kind of Love', 'Two Hearts' (both Phil Collins), 'Loco in Acapulco' (The Four Tops)*

Q7
Under the Cherry Moon

Q8
'Arthur's Theme (Best that You Can Do)'

Q9
G.I. Blues

Q10
Butch Cassidy and the Sundance Kid

QUESTION 1
Billed as 'special guest star', Gene Pitney appeared on which Marc Almond single that spent a month at number one in 1989?

QUESTION 2
Which female vocal group appeared alongside Earth Wind & Fire on their hit 'Boogie Wonderland'?

QUESTION 3
Miles Davis played trumpet on which hit single by Scritti Politti?

QUESTION 4
Which female singer featured alongside Maroon 5 on their international hit 'Moves Like Jagger'?

QUESTION 5
Neil Hannon of The Divine Comedy and Neil Tennant of the Pet Shop Boys both featured on backing vocals on which 1998 Robbie Williams single?

QUESTION 6
Which two of Michael Jackson's siblings are amongst the backing vocalists on his 1984 hit 'P.Y.T. (Pretty Young Thing)'?

QUESTION 7
Daft Punk's international number one 'Get Lucky' both featured and was co-written by Pharrell Williams and which guitarist?

QUESTION 8
Carl Wilson and Bruce Johnston of The Beach Boys sang backing vocals on which hit single from Elton John's 1974 album Caribou?

QUESTION 9
Which female R&B/hip-hop singer featured on Puff Daddy's 1997 worldwide number one 'I'll be Missing You'?

QUESTION 10
Which Donna Summer single features a backing choir that includes Lionel Richie, Dionne Warwick, Michael McDonald, Brenda Russell and Stevie Wonder?

POPMASTER QUIZ 088

GUEST STARRING (2)
Guest appearances by chart artists on other hit records... and beyond!

QUESTION 1
Who popped into the studio to add his backing vocals to Carly Simon's debut hit 'You're So Vain'?

QUESTION 2
What is the title of Sam Smith's 2015 number one that features American singer John Legend?

QUESTION 3
In which Australian TV programme did Chris Lowe of the Pet Shop Boys make a guest appearance in 1995?

QUESTION 4
Who was the guest guitarist on the 1986 number one remake of 'Living Doll' by Cliff Richard & The Young Ones?

QUESTION 5
Which actress, model and singer provided guest vocals on the Thompson Twins' 1983 hit 'Watching'?

QUESTION 6
Red Hot Chili Peppers, Paul McCartney, The White Stripes and the Ramones have all made guest appearances on which animated TV series?

QUESTION 7
Who was the guest lead guitarist on 'While My Guitar Gently Weeps', from The Beatles' White Album?

QUESTION 8
Lou Reed made a cameo appearance on a 1989 Top 20 single by Simple Minds. What was it called?

QUESTION 9
Which of these three singles by Tina Turner features a guest vocal from Sting – is it 'In Your Wildest Dreams', 'It's Only Love' or 'On Silent Wings'?

QUESTION 10
Which British group were guest stars in a 1986 episode of *The A-Team*?

Q1
David Bowie

Q2
The Trammps

Q3
'Because You Loved Me'

Q4
Ned Kelly

Q5
'Say You, Say Me'

Q6
Harry Connick Jr

Q7
Barbarella

Q8
8 Mile

Q9
Men In Black II

Q10
Jennifer Hudson

QUIZ 087
GUEST STARRING (1)

Q1
'Something's Gotten Hold of My Heart'

Q2
The Emotions

Q3
'Oh Patti (Don't Feel Sorry for Loverboy)'

Q4
Christina Aguilera

Q5
'No Regrets'

Q6
LaToya and Janet Jackson

Q7
Nile Rodgers

Q8
'Don't Let the Sun Go Down on Me'

Q9
Faith Evans

Q10
'State of Independence'

QUIZ 089 POPMASTER
HANDS

QUESTION 1
From 1957, what was the title of the only hit single achieved by Laurie London?

QUESTION 2
Which Birmingham-based band's second top ten hit from 1980 was called 'Hands Off - She's Mine'?

QUESTION 3
Topping the UK chart for five weeks in 1987, what was the title of the only number one hit for T'Pau?

QUESTION 4
Which singer enjoyed a number two hit in the UK in 1999 with 'If I Could Turn Back the Hands of Time'?

QUESTION 5
In 1972, which female duo made their top forty chart debut with a cover of Martha & The Vandellas' 'Third Finger, Left Hand'?

QUESTION 6
Can you name the first UK top ten hit achieved by Nine Inch Nails that made the singles chart in 2005?

QUESTION 7
Elton John achieved his first solo number one hit in the UK in 1990 with a double 'A'-sided hit that topped the chart for five weeks. One side was called 'Sacrifice', but what was the other song?

QUESTION 8
What was the name of the disco group that enjoyed a massive holiday hit in 1981 with 'Hands Up (Give Me Your Heart)'?

QUESTION 9
Can you give the title of the only major hit achieved in 1988 by UK act Breathe?

QUESTION 10
What were the names of the two children's TV entertainers who made the UK top twenty in 2000 with 'Hands Up'?

POPMASTER **QUIZ 090**

HEADS

QUESTION 1
What was the title of the debut hit and only top ten single achieved by the rock band Argent?

Q1
Mick Jagger

QUESTION 2
Jamaican reggae artist Clifford Smith achieved a top twenty hit in 1998 called 'Heads High'. Under what name did he release the single?

Q2
'Lay Me Down'

QUESTION 3
From 1965, what was the title of the only top forty hit achieved by Roy Head?

Q3
Neighbours

QUESTION 4
Can you name the female singer who topped the UK singles chart for four weeks in 2001 with 'Can't Get You out of My Head'?

Q4
Hank Marvin

QUESTION 5
Which group won a Grammy in 2003 for 'Best Alternative Album' with their classic release A Rush of Blood to the Head?

Q5
Grace Jones

QUESTION 6
In 1978, the Electric Light Orchestra achieved a top ten hit with their eponymous EP containing a song that gave them their first American top ten hit. Can you name it?

Q6
The Simpsons

QUESTION 7
In what year did the duo Kosheen achieve a UK top ten hit with 'All in My Head'?

Q7
Eric Clapton

QUESTION 8
Which group enjoyed the top twenty hit 'Head over Heels' in 1985, taken from their album Songs from the Big Chair?

Q8
'This is Your Land'

QUESTION 9
Name the act that topped the chart in 2009 with 'Killing in the Name', who made the top twenty in 1993 with 'Bullet in the Head'?

Q9
'On Silent Wings'

QUESTION 10
Owing much of their success to an early Eighties 'rowing boat' dance craze, which R&B group made their chart debut in 1980 with 'Oops Up Side Your Head'?

Q10
Culture Club (the episode was called Cowboy George)

Q1
'He's Got the Whole World in His Hands'

Q2
The Beat

Q3
'China in Your Hand'

Q4
R Kelly

Q5
The Pearls

Q6
'The Hand that Feeds'

Q7
'Healing Hands'

Q8
Ottawan

Q9
'Hands to Heaven'

Q10
Trevor and Simon

QUIZ 091 POPMASTER
HEALTH CARE

QUESTION 1
Which group featured Yazz & The Plastic Population on their debut hit single 'Doctorin' the House'?

QUESTION 2
Can you name the rock band that topped the American chart for two weeks in 1988 and made the UK top twenty with 'Bad Medicine'?

QUESTION 3
What was the title of the 1997 top twenty hit by Sly & Robbie that also featured Simply Red?

QUESTION 4
Which singer released a top twenty hit in 1983 called 'Pills and Soap' as Imposter?

QUESTION 5
In 1998, Danish group Aqua topped the UK chart for the second time with their follow-up record to 'Barbie Girl'. What was its title?

QUESTION 6
Which group included a song called 'Auto Surgery' on their 1993 top ten hit EP 'Shortsharpshock'?

QUESTION 7
Can you name the comedy star and actress whose record made the UK top five in 1960 inspired by, but not included in their movie *The Millionairess*? The single was titled 'Goodness Gracious Me'.

QUESTION 8
Which rock band released their third album in 1974 called Sheer Heart Attack?

QUESTION 9
Although they achieved several big hits in the Seventies and Eighties, Dr Hook only topped the UK singles chart on one occasion. Can you name the song?

QUESTION 10
What was the collective name of Paul Glancey and Duncan Glasson, who topped the UK chart in 1998 with 'Gym and Tonic'?

POPMASTER QUIZ 092
HERE COMES THE RAIN

QUESTION 1
In 1984, which duo made the UK top ten with their hit single 'Here Comes the Rain Again'?

QUESTION 2
Which successful Australian singer achieved a UK top ten hit in 1990 with a revival of The Cascades' 1963 hit 'Rhythm of the Rain'?

QUESTION 3
Following in the footsteps of 'Pearl's a Singer', whose second UK top ten hit in 1977 was called 'Sunshine After the Rain'?

QUESTION 4
Can you name the singer-songwriter whose 1966 recording of 'Rainy Day Women Nos. 12 & 35' made the UK top ten?

QUESTION 5
In 2008, which female singer embraced the UK chart with her top twenty hit 'Rain on Your Parade'?

QUESTION 6
With which American vocal group did Frankie Laine enjoy a UK top ten hit in 1954 with 'Rain, Rain, Rain'?

QUESTION 7
Which American singer-songwriter topped the American chart and scored a UK top twenty hit in 1974 with 'Laughter in the Rain'?

QUESTION 8
A year-and-a-half after their first top ten hit, which group achieved their second with 'Raincloud'?

QUESTION 9
Although not a major hit in the UK, which German act topped the American chart in 1989 with 'Blame it on the Rain'?

QUESTION 10
Which American female singer enjoyed a UK top twenty hit in 1981 with her hit single 'Rainy Night in Georgia'?

Q1
'Hold Your Head Up'

Q2
Mr Vegas

Q3
'Treat Her Right'

Q4
Kylie Minogue

Q5
Coldplay

Q6
'Can't Get it out of My Head'

Q7
2003

Q8
Tears for Fears

Q9
Rage Against the Machine

Q10
The Gap Band

answers

QUIZ 091
HEALTH CARE

Q1
Coldcut

Q2
Bon Jovi

Q3
'Night Nurse'

Q4
Elvis Costello

Q5
'Doctor Jones'

Q6
Therapy?

Q7
Peter Sellers and Sophia Loren

Q8
Queen

Q9
'When You're in Love with a Beautiful Woman'

Q10
Spacedust

QUIZ 093 POPMASTER
HERE COMES THE SUN

QUESTION 1
Name the singer who achieved his first solo UK top ten hit in 1973 with Bob Dylan's song 'A Hard Rain's Gonna Fall'.

QUESTION 2
Which band reached number one early in 1986 with 'The Sun Always Shines on TV'?

QUESTION 3
Can you name the male duo who achieved a UK top twenty hit in 2004 with 'The Sun has Come Your Way'?

QUESTION 4
Which group took George Harrison's song 'Here Comes the Sun' into the UK top ten in 1976?

QUESTION 5
What hit song title is shared on chart records by Gabrielle in 1999, Gareth Gates in 2003 and Twista in 2004?

QUESTION 6
Which group topped the UK chart for four weeks in 1966 with 'The Sun Ain't Gonna Shine Anymore'?

QUESTION 7
Can you name the male singer who achieved his first and only major UK hit in 2008 with 'Sun Goes Down'?

QUESTION 8
Which group first made the UK top twenty in 1968 with 'I Live for the Sun'?

QUESTION 9
What was the title of the 1999 top three UK hit by Bob Marley vs. Funkstar De Luxe?

QUESTION 10
Which legendary pop vocal duo achieved a 1962 UK top twenty hit with 'No One Can Make My Sunshine Smile'?

POPMASTER QUIZ 094

HOW GREEN IS YOUR GRASS?

QUESTION 1
Which legendary singer topped the singles chart for seven weeks in 1966 with 'Green, Green Grass of Home'?

QUESTION 2
Can you name the group that have never achieved UK chart success but made the American top ten with their hits 'Let's Live for Today', 'Midnight Confessions' and 'Sooner or Later'?

QUESTION 3
The Move's 1967 debut top ten hit was 'Night of Fear'. What was the second?

QUESTION 4
Which classic Ink Spots hit gave Windsor Davies and Don Estelle a three-week run at the top of the chart in 1975?

QUESTION 5
In 1967, which female singer made the top twenty with Tony Hatch's song 'The Other Man's Grass (Is Always Greener)'?

QUESTION 6
Which group made the top forty for the 13th and final time in 1969 with 'Snake in the Grass'?

QUESTION 7
Friends of Distinction achieved two top ten hits in America. One was 'Love or Let Me be Lonely' in 1970, but what was the title of the first from 1969?

QUESTION 8
In 1957, Johnny Duncan reached number two in the chart with 'Last Train to San Fernando'. What was the name of his backing group?

QUESTION 9
Which group sang about the 'Night of the Long Grass' on their 1967 top twenty hit?

QUESTION 10
Can you give the title of the only top 40 hit achieved in 1969 by vocal group Harmony Grass?

A nswers

QUIZ 092
HERE COMES THE RAIN

Q1
Eurythmics

Q2
Jason Donovan

Q3
Elkie Brooks

Q4
Bob Dylan

Q5
Duffy

Q6
The Four Lads

Q7
Neil Sedaka

Q8
The Lighthouse Family

Q9
Milli Vanilli

Q10
Randy Crawford

QUIZ 093
HERE COMES THE SUN

Q1
Bryan Ferry

Q2
A-ha

Q3
Sam & Mark

Q4
Steve Harley & Cockney Rebel

Q5
'Sunshine'

Q6
The Walker Brothers

Q7
David Jordan

Q8
Vanity Fare

Q9
'Sun is Shining'

Q10
The Everly Brothers

QUIZ 095 POPMASTER
I LOVE MY CAR

QUESTION 1
Which group achieved a top five hit in 1984 and again in 1985 with their song 'Drive'?

QUESTION 2
After his number one hit 'Are 'Friends' Electric?' with Tubeway Army, what was the title of Gary Numan's only other chart-topper?

QUESTION 3
What was the title of the album by The Beatles that first included their song 'Drive My Car' as the opening track?

QUESTION 4
Can you name the singer who topped the American chart for two weeks and made the UK top three with 'Get outta My Dreams Get into My Car'?

QUESTION 5
What was the title of the only top forty hit credited to Paul & Linda McCartney?

QUESTION 6
Acccording to their top ten hit from 2006 and 2007, which group were 'Chasing Cars'?

QUESTION 7
Which American singer won a Grammy in 1988 for her only UK top five hit, 'Fast Car'?

QUESTION 8
In 2005, which legendary singer recorded the UK top twenty hit 'What Car'?

QUESTION 9
Which group achieved their 11th UK top ten hit with 'Driving in My Car'?

QUESTION 10
Under what name did performer Paul Phillips release his only UK top ten hit, 'Car 67', in 1978?

POPMASTER QUIZ 096
I SEE THE LIGHT

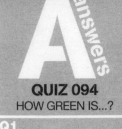

QUESTION 1
Which successful drummer, composer and singer achieved his final top ten hit of the Nineties with 'Dance into the Light'?

Q1
Tom Jones

QUESTION 2
What hit song has been successfully recorded by The Doors, Jose Feliciano and Will Young?

Q2
The Grass Roots

QUESTION 3
Who wrote Manfred Mann's Earth Band's 1976 American number one and UK top ten hit 'Blinded by the Light'?

Q3
'I Can Hear the Grass Grow'

QUESTION 4
Which legendary rock 'n' roll performer scored a UK top twenty hit in 1959 with 'By the Light of the Silvery Moon'?

Q4
'Whispering Grass'

QUESTION 5
In 2005, which American female rapper achieved a UK top twenty hit with her hit record 'Lighters Up'?

Q5
Petula Clark

QUESTION 6
Can you name the Romanian panpipe player who scored a 1976 UK top five hit with the instrumental theme music to the TV series *The Light of Experience* called '(Light of Experience) Doina de Jale'?

Q6
Dave Dee, Dozy, Beaky, Mick & Tich

QUESTION 7
After the success of her 1970 Eurovision Song Contest and number one hit 'All Kinds of Everything', Dana had to wait nearly a year for her next top twenty hit. Can you name it?

Q7
'Grazing in the Grass'

QUESTION 8
Which one-time member of the group Eternal achieved her first solo hit in 1995 with 'Light of My Life'?

Q8
The Blue Grass Boys

QUESTION 9
Scott Walker achieved two solo top twenty hits in the Sixties - the first was 'Joanna', what was the second?

Q9
The Troggs

QUESTION 10
The daughter of Elvis Presley, Lisa Marie Presley, achieved a UK top twenty hit in 2003. What was the title?

Q10
'Move in a Little Closer Baby'

QUIZ 095
I LOVE MY CAR

Q1
The Cars

Q2
'Cars'

Q3
Rubber Soul

Q4
Billy Ocean

Q5
'Back Seat of My Car'

Q6
Snow Patrol

Q7
Tracy Chapman

Q8
Cliff Richard

Q9
Madness

Q10
Driver 67

QUESTION 1
What are the names of the two-man songwriting team behind the biggest hits for The Sweet, Mud and Suzi Quatro?

QUESTION 2
Which superstar has written songs under the names Alexander Nevermind, Joey Coco and 'Symbol'?

QUESTION 3
Which successful singer bucked the trend by choosing to sing an original song when she first auditioned for *The X Factor* in 2012?

QUESTION 4
The singer-songwriter who won the BBC's *Fame Academy* and reached number one with 'Stop Living the Lie' has gone on to write for Matt Cardle, Hurts, Lana Del Rey, Morten Harket and Newton Faulkner. Who is he?

QUESTION 5
One of America's most successful female songwriters penned 'How Do I Live' for LeAnn Rimes, 'I Don't Want to Miss a Thing' for Aerosmith and 'Because You Loved Me' for Celine Dion. Who is she?

QUESTION 6
Who is Chris Difford's songwriting partner on the Squeeze hit singles?

QUESTION 7
What is the name of the legendary New York building that was the songwriting 'office' to Carole King, Neil Sedaka, Gerry Goffin and Johnny Mercer, amongst others?

QUESTION 8
The 1998 album Painted from Memory was a collaboration between two hugely successful songwriters. Who are they?

QUESTION 9
What are the first names of the successful Motown writing partnership of Ashford and Simpson?

QUESTION 10
Who actually wrote the Barry Manilow signature song 'I Write the Songs' – was it Stephen Sondheim, Bruce Johnston of The Beach Boys, David Cassidy or Dewey Bunnell of America?

POPMASTER QUIZ 098
IFS AND BUTS

QUESTION 1
Which legendary American country singer achieved a top twenty hit in 1969 with 'But You Love Me Daddy'?

QUESTION 2
Can you name the husband and wife duo who achieved a UK top twenty hit in 1965 with 'But You're Mine'?

QUESTION 3
Can you name the female singer who made her UK chart debut in 1971 with Bob Dylan's song 'If Not for You'?

QUESTION 4
Which successful American group achieved a UK top ten hit in 1976 with 'If Not You'?

QUESTION 5
Can you name the successful vocal duo who achieved a top twenty hit in 1999 with 'I Don't Know What You Want but I Can't Give it Anymore'?

QUESTION 6
Which American country singer scored a UK top twenty hit in 2002 with 'But I Do Love You'?

QUESTION 7
What was the title of Clarence 'Frogman' Henry's first UK hit from 1961?

QUESTION 8
Can you name the Irish singer who sadly passed away in 2015, who after changing record labels from Decca to Pye in 1967 scored a top three hit with 'If the Whole World Stopped Lovin"?

QUESTION 9
Daniel Bedingfield topped the singles chart in late 2001 and again in early 2002 with 'Gotta Get Thru This', but what was the title of his next number one single?

QUESTION 10
Which British actor and singer achieved a top five hit in 1960 with his hit recording of 'If She Should Come to You?

Q1
Phil Collins

Q2
'Light My Fire'

Q3
Bruce Springsteen

Q4
Little Richard

Q5
Lil' Kim

Q6
Gheorghe Zamfir

Q7
'Who Put the Lights Out'

Q8
Louise

Q9
'Lights of Cincinnati'

Q10
'Lights Out'

QUIZ 097
I WRITE THE SONGS

Q1
Nicky Chinn and Mike Chapman

Q2
Prince

Q3
Ella Henderson

Q4
David Sneddon

Q5
Diane Warren

Q6
Glenn Tilbrook

Q7
Brill Building

Q8
Elvis Costello and Burt Bacharach

Q9
Nickolas and Valerie

Q10
Bruce Johnston

QUIZ 099 POPMASTER
IN ORDER (1)

In each case, and beginning with the earliest, put these three songs by each group or artist in the order they were originally UK Top 40 hits

QUESTION 1
Billy Joel - 'The River of Dreams', 'The Longest Time', 'My Life'

QUESTION 2
Elvis Presley - 'Suspicious Minds', 'Wooden Heart', 'Suspicion'

QUESTION 3
Texas - 'Getaway', 'Black Eyed Boy', 'I Don't Want a Lover'

QUESTION 4
Take That - 'Rule the World', 'These Days', 'Back for Good'

QUESTION 5
Rod Stewart - 'Young Turks', 'Downtown Train', 'Oh! No Not My Baby'

QUESTION 6
Kim Wilde - 'Chequered Love', 'Love is Holy', 'You Came'

QUESTION 7
Blur - 'Tender', 'Girls and Boys', 'Under the Westway'

QUESTION 8
Madonna - 'Jump', 'Rain', 'Angel'

QUESTION 9
George Michael - 'Spinning the Wheel', 'One More Try', 'Amazing'

QUESTION 10
Status Quo - 'Rollin' Home', 'Whatever You Want', 'Paper Plane'

POPMASTER QUIZ 100

IN ORDER (2)

In each case, and beginning with the earliest, put these three songs by each group or artist in the order they were originally UK Top 40 hits

QUESTION 1
Duran Duran - '(Reach Up for the) Sunrise', 'Ordinary World', 'Notorious'

QUESTION 2
Janet Jackson - 'All for You', 'Runaway','Let's Wait Awhile'

QUESTION 3
Paul McCartney - 'Young Boy', 'Once Upon a Long Ago', 'Coming Up'

QUESTION 4
Will Young - 'Jealousy', 'Don't Let Me Down', 'All Time Love'

QUESTION 5
The Rolling Stones - 'Mixed Emotions', 'Miss You', 'Let's Spend the Night Together'

QUESTION 6
Simply Red - 'Sunrise', 'Fairground', 'The Right Thing'

QUESTION 7
Diana Ross - 'One Shining Moment', 'All of My Life', 'Work that Body'

QUESTION 8
Oasis - 'Go Let it Out', 'Some Might Say', 'The Importance of Being Idle'

QUESTION 9
Lady Gaga - 'Applause', 'Just Dance', 'The Edge of Glory'

QUESTION 10
David Bowie - 'Jump They Say', 'Blue Jean', 'Heroes'

Q1
Jim Reeves

Q2
Sonny & Cher

Q3
Olivia Newton-John

Q4
Dr Hook

Q5
Pet Shop Boys

Q6
LeAnn Rimes

Q7
'But I Do'

Q8
Val Doonican

Q9
'If You're Not the One'

Q10
Anthony Newley

Q1
'My Life' ('78), 'The Longest Time' ('84), 'The River of Dreams' ('93)

Q2
'Wooden Heart' ('61), 'Suspicious Minds' ('69), 'Suspicion' ('76)

Q3
'I Don't Want a Lover' ('89), 'Black Eyed Boy' ('97), 'Getaway' ('05)

Q4
'Back for Good' ('95), 'Rule the World' ('07), 'These Days' ('14)

Q5
'Oh! No Not My Baby' ('73), 'Young Turks' ('81), 'Downtown Train' ('90)

Q6
'Chequered Love' ('81), 'You Came' ('88), 'Love is Holy' ('92)

Q7
'Girls and Boys' ('94), 'Tender' ('99), 'Under the Westway' ('12)

Q8
'Angel' ('85), 'Rain' ('93), 'Jump' ('06)

Q9
'One More Try' ('88), 'Spinning the Wheel' ('96), 'Amazing' ('04)

Q10
'Paper Plane' ('73), 'Whatever You Want' ('79), 'Rollin' Home' ('86)

QUIZ 101 POPMASTER
INSTRUMENTAL HITS
Simply name the chart acts that had these hits, all classed as instrumentals

QUESTION 1
'Frankenstein' (1973)

QUESTION 2
'The Groove' (1980)

QUESTION 3
'The Man in Black' (1974)

QUESTION 4
'Side Saddle' (1959)

QUESTION 5
'Footsee' (1975)

QUESTION 6
'Tired of Getting Pushed Around' (1988)

QUESTION 7
'Oxygene Part IV' (1977)

QUESTION 8
'Infinity' (1990)/'Infinity 2008' (2008)

QUESTION 9
'Toccata' (1980)

QUESTION 10
'Keep Your Eye on Me' (1987)

POPMASTER QUIZ 102

IT'S A SIGN

QUESTION 1
Released in 1967, whose only top ten hit was 'Gimme Little Sign'?

QUESTION 2
Which of his hit songs did Stevie Wonder revive in 2003 when he was featured with Angie Stone on the top twenty hit by Blue?

QUESTION 3
Can you name the only top ten hit achieved by girl group The Belle Stars in 1983?

QUESTION 4
Terence Trent D'Arby achieved three top ten hits in the Eighties with 'If You Let Me Stay', 'Wishing Well' and which other single?

QUESTION 5
Which long-running music radio show features a piece of music called 'At the Sign of the Swinging Cymbal' as its signature tune?

QUESTION 6
Also the title track of his first solo album following the departure of his backing band, who achieved a top ten hit in 1987 with 'Sign o' the Times'?

QUESTION 7
Can you name the legendary female Tamla Motown group who achieved a top forty hit in 1969 with 'No Matter What Sign You Are'?

QUESTION 8
From 2003, can you name the only top twenty hit by studio group Kontakt?

QUESTION 9
Following 'All that She Wants', which Swedish group achieved their second top three hit in 1994 with 'The Sign'?

QUESTION 10
Which male rapper reached number two in 2005 with his hit 'Signs', featuring Charlie Wilson and Justin Timberlake?

QUIZ 100
IN ORDER (2)

Q1
'Notorious' ('86), 'Ordinary World' ('93), '(Reach Up for the) Sunrise' ('04)

Q2
'Let's Wait Awhile' ('87), 'Runaway' ('95), 'All for You' ('01)

Q3
'Coming Up' ('80), 'Once Upon a Long Ago' ('87), 'Young Boy' ('97)

Q4
'Don't Let Me Down' ('02), 'All Time Love' ('06), 'Jealousy' ('11)

Q5
'Let's Spend the Night Together' ('67), 'Miss You' ('78), 'Mixed Emotions' ('89)

Q6
'The Right Thing' ('87), 'Fairground' ('95), 'Sunrise' ('03)

Q7
'All of My Life' ('74), 'Work that Body' ('82), 'One Shining Moment' ('92)

Q8
'Some Might Say' ('95), 'Go Let it Out' ('00), 'The Importance of Being Idle' ('05)

Q9
'Just Dance' ('09), 'The Edge of Glory' ('11), 'Applause' ('13)

Q10
'Heroes' ('77), 'Blue Jean' ('84), 'Jump They Say' ('93)

QUIZ 103 POPMASTER
IT'S BED TIME

QUESTION 1
What was the title of the UK top five novelty hit of the Eighties by Morris Minor & The Majors?

QUESTION 2
Which successful vocal group achieved an American top ten hit in 1972 with Tony Macaulay's song '(Last Night) I Didn't Get to Sleep at All'?

QUESTION 3
Can you name the Australian band that achieved their only UK top ten hit in 1989 with 'Beds are Burning'?

QUESTION 4
Ray Parker Jr achieved two UK top twenty hits in the Eighties - the first was 'Ghostbusters', but what was the title of the other?

QUESTION 5
Which trio consisting of Tom Chaplin, Richard Hughes and Tim Rice-Oxley achieved a 2004 top ten hit with 'Bedshaped'?

QUESTION 6
Can you name the successful group that achieved a top twenty hit in the UK in 1968 with 'Sleepy Joe'?

QUESTION 7
What was the title of Madonna's 1995 top ten hit written by Björk, Nellee Hooper and Marius de Vries?

QUESTION 8
Name the instrumental duo that topped the American chart and made the UK top forty in 1959 with 'Sleep Walk'.

QUESTION 9
In 1967, which successful female artist said 'Don't Sleep in the Subway'?

QUESTION 10
Which 1993 top twenty hit by Bon Jovi begins with the lines "Sitting here wasted and wounded at this old piano, trying hard to capture the moment this morning I don't know."

POPMASTER QUIZ 104

IT'S TEA TIME

QUESTION 1
Can you name the American pop group that made the top twenty in 1964 with 'Bread and Butter'?

QUESTION 2
Released in 1980, what was the title of the only top forty hit achieved by R&B group Coffee?

QUESTION 3
Which group made the top twenty for the first of many times in 1977 with their hit 'All Around the World'?

QUESTION 4
Can you name the band that won a 1999 MTV award for 'Best Video' for their hit song 'Coffee + TV'?

QUESTION 5
From 1978, which group featuring Paul Young on vocals achieved their only hit with their double 'A'-sided hit 'Toast' and 'Hold On'?

QUESTION 6
What was the title of the 1958 top three hit by Tommy Dorsey & His Orchestra starring Warren Covington?

QUESTION 7
In 2002, which legendary rock band was back in the top twenty with their recording of 'Jam Side Down'?

QUESTION 8
Can you name the group that topped the chart for a total of three weeks at the beginning of 1969 with Lennon and McCartney's 'Ob-La-Di, Ob-La-Da'?

QUESTION 9
In 1970, which singer-songwriter released his successful album Tea for the Tillerman?

QUESTION 10
Which American band made their chart debut in 1997 with 'The Distance'?

Q1
Brenton Wood

Q2
'Signed, Sealed, Delivered, I'm Yours'

Q3
'Sign of the Times'

Q4
'Sign Your Name'

Q5
Pick of the Pops

Q6
Prince

Q7
Diana Ross & The Supremes

Q8
'Show Me a Sign'

Q9
Ace of Base

Q10
Snoop Dogg

QUIZ 105 POPMASTER
JOE MEEK PRODUCTIONS

Q1
'Stutter Rap (No Sleep 'Til Bedtime)'

Q2
The 5th Dimension

Q3
Midnight Oil

Q4
'I Don't Think that Man Should Sleep Alone'

Q5
Keane

Q6
Herman's Hermits

Q7
'Bedtime Story'

Q8
Santo and Johnny

Q9
Petula Clark

Q10
'Bed of Roses'

QUESTION 1
The Honeycombs achieved two UK top twenty hits in the Sixties, the first being their number one 'Have I the Right'. What was the title of the other?

QUESTION 2
What was the name of the short-lived but successful label formed by Joe Meek in the early Sixties?

QUESTION 3
The biggest hit on the label Joe Meek formed was the 1960 UK top ten hit by Michael Cox - what was the title?

QUESTION 4
An international hit for Joe Meek was the 1962 UK and American number one 'Telstar', recorded by which successful instrumental group?

QUESTION 5
Which one-time member of the group that recorded 'Telstar' achieved his only top ten hit in 1963 with his tribute to Eddie Cochran, titled 'Just Like Eddie'?

QUESTION 6
In 1961, which male vocalist made the UK top forty with his debut hit produced by Joe Meek, 'Tribute to Buddy Holly'?

QUESTION 7
A much sought-after and requested record today is the 1966 top forty hit by The Cryin' Shames. Can you name it?

QUESTION 8
Can you name the singer who appeared with Lulu in the 1965 movie Gonks Go Beat and achieved a UK top forty hit in 1962 with 'Can't You Hear the Beat of a Broken Heart'?

QUESTION 9
Can you name the group who made the UK top forty in 1960 with their instrumental hit 'Green Jeans', based on the traditional folk song 'Greensleeves'?

QUESTION 10
Which actor achieved a number one hit in 1961 with a song that was featured in the TV series *Harpers West One*, 'Johnny Remember Me'?

POPMASTER QUIZ 106
KEEP ON DREAMING

QUIZ 104
IT'S TEA TIME

QUESTION 1
Which group enjoyed a week at the top of the American chart and a first major UK hit in 1983 with 'Sweet Dreams (Are Made of This)'?

QUESTION 2
Can you name the American group that topped the UK chart for three weeks in 1956 with 'It's Almost Tomorrow'?

QUESTION 3
In 1979, which hugely successful male and female group had a Christmas top three hit in the UK with 'I Have a Dream'?

QUESTION 4
'Dream On' was the first top ten hit of the Noughties for which successful Essex group?

QUESTION 5
What is the common name of the group that made the top ten in 1974 with 'Honey Honey' and the act that performed the 1983 UK entry into the Eurovision Song Contest, 'I'm Never Giving Up'?

QUESTION 6
What was the collective name of the UK male production trio Paul Spencer, Scott Rosser and Stephen Spencer, who made the top ten in 2001 with 'Dream to Me'?

QUESTION 7
In 1961, which legendary pop star made the UK top three with his hit single 'Theme for a Dream'?

QUESTION 8
Can you name the trio who achieved their only UK top twenty hit in 1985 with 'Life in a Northern Town'?

QUESTION 9
Which American singer topped the UK singles chart for four weeks in 1959 with 'Dream Lover'?

QUESTION 10
What was the title of the debut UK top ten hit in 2007 by vocalist and guitarist Newton Faulkner?

Answers

Q1
The Newbeats

Q2
'Casanova'

Q3
The Jam

Q4
Blur

Q5
Streetband

Q6
'Tea for Two Cha-Cha'

Q7
Status Quo

Q8
Marmalade

Q9
Cat Stevens

Q10
Cake

Q1
'That's the Way'

Q2
Triumph

Q3
'Angela Jones'

Q4
The Tornados

Q5
Heinz

Q6
Mike Berry (billed as Mike Berry with The Outlaws)

Q7
'Please Stay'

Q8
Iain Gregory

Q9
The Flee-Rekkers

Q10
John Leyton

QUIZ 107 POPMASTER
LEFT AND RIGHT

QUESTION 1
Which legendary singer achieved a UK top forty hit in 1958 with 'I'm Left, You're Right, She's Gone'?

QUESTION 2
Can you name the duo who achieved their 11th consecutive top twenty hit in 1988 with 'Left to My Own Devices'?

QUESTION 3
Can you name the hit song title that was shared between The Creatures in 1983, Atomic Kitten in 1999 and Akon in 2008?

QUESTION 4
From 1999, can you name the performer who was once a member of The Housemartins, formed Beats International, and reached number two in the UK with 'Right Here, Right Now'?

QUESTION 5
Which male vocalist was featured playing piano on Suzanne Vega's 1986 top forty hit 'Left of Center'?

QUESTION 6
By what collective name are Frankee Connolly and Britt Love - who made the UK top ten in 2009 with 'I Left My Heart in Tokyo' - better known?

QUESTION 7
What was the title of Sinitta's 1989 top ten hit that was a revival of Maxine Nightingale's 1975 original?

QUESTION 8
Can you name the American rapper who achieved his first UK number one in 2009 with 'Right Round'?

QUESTION 9
In 1989, Richard Marx achieved his biggest UK hit, reaching number two with a song that topped the American chart for three weeks. What was the title?

QUESTION 10
Which group achieved a top twenty hit in 1998 with 'She Left Me on Friday'?

POPMASTER QUIZ 108

LISTEN TO THE BANNED

These are questions about records that have been refused play by one organization or another, for whatever reasons they felt necessary

QUESTION 1
Whilst presenting BBC Radio 1's breakfast show in the Eighties, which Frankie Goes to Hollywood record did Mike Read refuse to play on the grounds of its references to carnal knowledge?

QUESTION 2
Many football grounds refused to play 'Glad all Over' by The Dave Clark Five. Can you offer a reason why?

QUESTION 3
Which group had a 1997 top ten hit that many radio stations refused to play for obvious reasons - the song was called 'Smack My Bitch Up'?

QUESTION 4
Which 1970 number two hit by The Kinks required a line about Coca-Cola being changed to cherry-cola to avoid advertising?

QUESTION 5
In 2007, controversy reigned over the re-issue of a single by The Pogues featuring the late Kirsty MacColl. Radio 1 refused to play it unless certain words were edited out. After many complaints, the ban was revoked. What was the song?

QUESTION 6
In 1967, DJ Simon Dee was instructed not to play Scott Walker's first solo hit on his show because of the lyrical content. He ignored the instruction and was suspended from the programme. What was the title of the offending song?

QUESTION 7
'Johnny Remember Me' by John Leyton, 'Moody River' by Pat Boone and 'Terry' by Twinkle were just three records that caused the BBC concern for the same reason - what was it?

QUESTION 8
A record by Lil Louis caused an outcry from radio stations in 1989 because of its sexual overtones, but despite many not playing it the record reached number two in the UK. What was the title?

QUESTION 9
The Stranglers' first top ten hit from 1977 was a double 'A' side. One of the songs was 'Go Buddy Go'. What was the title of the other side, which failed to receive plays because of the lyrical content?

QUESTION 10
Why were the BBC reluctant to play the Sixties instrumental hits 'Nut Rocker' by B Bumble & The Stingers, 'Saturday Night at the Duck Pond' by The Cougars and 'Can Can '62' by Peter Jay & The Jaywalkers?

QUIZ 106
KEEP ON DREAMING

Q1
Eurythmics

Q2
The Dreamweavers

Q3
ABBA

Q4
Depeche Mode

Q5
Sweet Dreams

Q6
Dario G

Q7
Cliff Richard

Q8
Dream Academy

Q9
Bobby Darin

Q10
'Dream Catch Me'

111

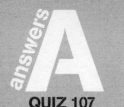

QUIZ 107
LEFT AND RIGHT

Q1
Elvis Presley

Q2
Pet Shop Boys

Q3
'Right Now'

Q4
Fatboy Slim

Q5
Joe Jackson

Q6
Mini Viva

Q7
'Right Back Where We Started From'

Q8
Flo Rida

Q9
'Right Here Waiting'

Q10
Shed Seven

QUIZ 109 POPMASTER
LITERARY POP

QUESTION 1
The 1995 Top 10 song 'Wake Up Boo!' was the biggest hit for The Boo Radleys, who took their name from which book?

QUESTION 2
Named after the fictional band in *A Clockwork Orange* by Anthony Burgess, Heaven 17 had their biggest hit in 1983 with which Top 3 song?

QUESTION 3
Who was the mastermind songwriter and producer behind the musical version of *The War of the Worlds* in the late Seventies?

QUESTION 4
Ian Dury recorded the song 'Profoundly in Love with Pandora' as the theme song to a 1985 TV adaptation of which Sue Townsend book?

QUESTION 5
Which duo provided the musical soundtrack to the film version of George Orwell's *1984*, starring John Hurt?

QUESTION 6
Which Neil Diamond song, recorded by Urge Overkill, was a Top 40 hit having been featured in Quentin Tarantino's film *Pulp Fiction*?

QUESTION 7
Though not a hit single, which famous song by Jefferson Airplane references the work of Lewis Carroll?

QUESTION 8
Which musical by Andrew Lloyd Webber is closely linked to the work of T.S. Eliot?

QUESTION 9
'Lovefool' by The Cardigans, 'Talk Show Host' by Radiohead and Kym Mazelle's version of 'Young Hearts Run Free' all featured on the soundtrack album to which Baz Luhrmann-directed film?

QUESTION 10
Which British rock band that had a run of chart albums in the Seventies and early Eighties takes its name from a character in Charles Dickens' *David Copperfield*?

POPMASTER QUIZ 110

LIVE AID

Live Aid happened 30 years ago this year. How good is your memory?

QUESTION 1
Which group opened the 1985 Live Aid concert?

QUESTION 2
Madonna and Nile Rodgers joined the Thompson Twins on stage in Philadelphia for a version of which Beatles song?

QUESTION 3
Thomas Dolby played keyboards at Wembley for which superstar's set?

QUESTION 4
Who performed on both the London and Philadelphia stages?

QUESTION 5
Who was the only female act to play a full set on the Wembley stage?

QUESTION 6
Former Temptations members Eddie Kendricks and David Ruffin joined one of America's most successful duos on stage in Philadelphia. Name the duo.

QUESTION 7
While most of Live Aid's London acts performed well-known hits, who came on stage and performed his upcoming single 'Vive le Rock'?

QUESTION 8
Who performed a medley of 'Amazing Grace' and 'We Are the World' in Philadelphia?

QUESTION 9
Elton John had both a female and male guest singer during his set. Name both of them.

QUESTION 10
Which one-time Radio 1 DJ made the famous opening PA announcement at Live Aid?

Q1
'Relax'

Q2
Fans stomped their feet to the beat, causing concern that the stands might collapse

Q3
The Prodigy

Q4
'Lola'

Q5
'Fairytale of New York'

Q6
'Jackie'

Q7
They are all about death

Q8
'French Kiss'

Q9
'Peaches'

Q10
They were offended by tunes based on classical themes that were given a pop treatment

QUIZ 109
LITERARY POP

Q1
To Kill a Mockingbird *by Harper Lee*

Q2
'Temptation'

Q3
Jeff Wayne

Q4
The Secret Diary of Adrian Mole Aged 13 3/4

Q5
Eurythmics

Q6
'Girl, You'll be a Woman Soon'

Q7
'White Rabbit'

Q8
Cats

Q9
Romeo and Juliet

Q10
Uriah Heep

QUIZ 111 POPMASTER

LONG PLAYERS

Questions relating to songs that have spent at least six weeks as the UK's number one single

QUESTION 1
Which film featured Wet Wet Wet's 15-week number one 'Love is All Around'?

QUESTION 2
Which of Frankie Goes to Hollywood's singles spent the longest at number one?

QUESTION 3
Released in 1962 and with eight weeks at number one, name both the group and the title of the UK's most successful instrumental chart-topper.

QUESTION 4
Which rapper featured as a guest on Rihanna's 2007 10-week number one 'Umbrella'?

QUESTION 5
One of the co-writers of The Archies' eight-week number one 'Sugar, Sugar' is Andy Kim, who went on to have his own Top 3 single in 1974. What was that called?

QUESTION 6
Who is the frontman of the group Mungo Jerry, who wrote the band's 1970 number one 'In the Summertime'?

QUESTION 7
In 1956, 'Just Walking in the Rain' spent seven weeks at number one for a singer who is name-checked in the lyrics of 'Come on Eileen' by Dexy's Midnight Runners. Who is he?

QUESTION 8
Stevie Wonder's six-week number one 'I Just Called to Say I Love You' featured in a 1984 romantic comedy starring Gene Wilder and Kelly LeBrock. What was it called?

QUESTION 9
Who is the vocalist on Gnarls Barkley's 'Crazy', which spent nine weeks at number one in 2006?

QUESTION 10
Queen's 'Bohemian Rhapsody' spent nine consecutive weeks at number one in 1975-1976. It was knocked off the top by an ABBA single whose title is contained within 'Bohemian Rhapsody's lyrics. What is that ABBA song?

POPMASTER QUIZ 112

MAGNETIC MUSIC
Questions about the hit record label Magnet Records

QUIZ 110
LIVE AID

QUESTION 1
The label's co-founder wrote the majority of Alvin Stardust's hits on the label and reached the chart himself with 'Gee Baby' and 'Love Me Love My Dog'. Who is he?

QUESTION 2
...and in 1974, Alvin Stardust had his only UK number one with his second hit single on the label. What was it called?

QUESTION 3
The 1983 Top 20 single 'Last Film' was the only chart hit for the group Kissing the... what?

QUESTION 4
Which vocal group released the hit singles 'There's a Whole Lot of Loving' and 'You Don't Have to Say You Love Me' on the label in the mid-Seventies?

QUESTION 5
The ska-flavoured band Bad Manners had a run of hits on Magnet in the early Eighties. What is the name of their lead singer?

QUESTION 6
Darts had three consecutive number two hits on Magnet in 1978 – 'The Boy from New York City' was the middle of these three, but can you name one of the other two?

QUESTION 7
Which group had Top 10 hits on the label in the mid-Nineties called 'U R the Best Thing' (remix) and 'Shoot Me with Your Love'?

QUESTION 8
The singles 'Rockabilly Rebel' and a medley of 'Over the Rainbow – You Belong to Me' were the first and last of five Top 40 hits on the label for the group Matchbox. Name one of the other three.

QUESTION 9
MAG 111 was the record number of Chris Rea's chart debut in 1978. What was the title of this first hit single for him?

QUESTION 10
'Cry Boy Cry' was a hit for the label in 1982. Which group recorded it?

Q1 *Status Quo (though the Coldstream Guards had performed the National Anthem before this)*

Q2 *'Revolution'*

Q3 *David Bowie*

Q4 *Phil Collins*

Q5 *Sade*

Q6 *Daryl Hall and John Oates*

Q7 *Adam Ant*

Q8 *Joan Baez*

Q9 *Kiki Dee ('Don't Go Breaking My Heart'), George Michael ('Don't Let the Sun Go Down on Me')*

Q10 *Richard Skinner*

Q1
Four Weddings and a Funeral

Q2
'Two Tribes' (nine consecutive weeks in 1984)

Q3
The Shadows – 'Wonderful Land'

Q4
Jay Z

Q5
'Rock Me Gently'

Q6
Ray Dorset

Q7
Johnnie Ray

Q8
The Woman in Red

Q9
CeeLo Green

Q10
'Mamma Mia'

QUIZ 113 POPMASTER
MICKIE MOST PRODUCTIONS

QUESTION 1
What was the title of the 1970 top three UK hit that was placed second in the Eurovision Song Contest that year, performed by Mary Hopkin and produced by Mickie Most?

QUESTION 2
What was the title of the 1969 top three UK hit that was placed joint winner with three other countries in the Eurovision Song Contest that year, performed by Lulu and produced by Mickie Most?

QUESTION 3
Who was the singer who formed the group C.C.S. and achieved their first hit in 1970 with a cover of Led Zeppelin's 'Whole Lotta Love'?

QUESTION 4
What was the title of the only number one hit by The Animals that topped both the UK and American charts in 1964?

QUESTION 5
Which group featured on Donovan's 1969 UK top twenty hit 'Goo Goo Barabajagal (Love is Hot)'?

QUESTION 6
Which British group scored American number one hits in America in 1965 with 'Mrs Brown You've Got a Lovely Daughter' and 'I'm Henry VIII, I Am', neither of which were released as singles in the UK?

QUESTION 7
Written by Kenny Young, who had a top forty hit with the Mickie Most production of 'The Highway Song'?

QUESTION 8
Mickie Most produced a top twenty hit for Brenda Lee in the Sixties whilst she was visiting the UK. Was it 'Losing You', 'Is it True' or 'It Started all Over Again'?

QUESTION 9
Which well-established folk singer achieved her only UK top twenty hit in 1970 with a cover of Paul Simon's 'If I Could (El Condor Pasa)'?

QUESTION 10
Can you name the group that achieved two top ten hits in 1964 with 'Tobacco Road' and 'Google Eye', both written by John D Loudermilk?

POPMASTER QUIZ 114
MONTHS OF THE YEAR

QUIZ 112
MAGNETIC MUSIC

QUESTION 1
'December Will be Magic Again' was a Christmas hit in 1980 for whom?

Q1
Peter Shelley

QUESTION 2
What type of '...Rain' featured in the title of a 1992 Top 5 single by Guns N' Roses?

Q2
'Jealous Mind'

QUESTION 3
Which month of the year did Earth Wind & Fire sing about in 1978?

Q3
Pink

QUESTION 4
Which member of Queen reached the Top 10 in 1992 with 'Too Much Love Will Kill You'?

Q4
Guys 'N' Dolls

QUESTION 5
The 1991 single 'Winter in July' was the fourth and final Top 10 hit for UK producer Tim Simenon, recording under what name?

Q5
Buster Bloodvessel

QUESTION 6
Which singer-songwriter released a live double album in the early Seventies called Hot August Night?

Q6
'Come Back My Love', 'It's Raining'

QUESTION 7
Which month of the year provided the title of the only number one single by Pilot?

Q7
D:Ream

QUESTION 8
Released in 1987, the song 'April Skies' was the first Top 10 hit by the band formed by brothers Jim and William Reid. What are they called?

Q8
'Buzz Buzz a Diddle It', 'Midnite Dynamos', 'When You Ask About Love'

QUESTION 9
The U2 singles 'Fire' and 'Gloria' featured on the second studio album by U2. What was it called?

Q9
'Fool (If You Think it's Over)'

QUESTION 10
In 1977, the Trinidad Oil Company had its only chart hit with a song subtitled '(January, February, March, April, May)'. What was it called?

Q10
Blue Zoo

QUIZ 113
MICKIE MOST PRODUCTIONS

Q1
'Knock Knock Who's There'

Q2
'Boom Bang-a-Bang'

Q3
Alexis Korner

Q4
'The House of the Rising Sun'

Q5
The Jeff Beck Group

Q6
Herman's Hermits

Q7
Nancy Sinatra

Q8
'Is it True'

Q9
Julie Felix

Q10
The Nashville Teens

QUIZ 115 POPMASTER
NAME THE ALBUM

For each question, name the artist and the studio album that contains these songs. An extra point if you also know the year of the album's release!

QUESTION 1
'Another Part of Me', 'Liberian Girl', 'Smooth Criminal'

QUESTION 2
'I Predict a Riot', 'Modern Way', 'Oh My God'

QUESTION 3
'Satellite of Love', 'Perfect Day', 'Walk on the Wild Side'

QUESTION 4
'Eleanor Rigby', 'And Your Bird Can Sing', 'Good Day Sunshine'

QUESTION 5
'Country House', 'Charmless Man', 'The Universal'

QUESTION 6
'Private Investigations', 'Telegraph Road', 'Industrial Disease'

QUESTION 7
'Shake it Off', 'Blank Space', 'Welcome to New York'

QUESTION 8
'Walking on the Moon', 'Bed's Too Big Without You', 'Bring on the Night'

QUESTION 9
'Baba O'Reilly', 'Behind Blue Eyes', 'Won't Get Fooled Again'

QUESTION 10
'Warwick Avenue', 'Stepping Stone', 'Mercy'

POPMASTER QUIZ 116

NOT ON THIS ALBUM

Ten number one albums and their artists are listed along with three songs, one of which was not on the album. Can you spot the bogus track?

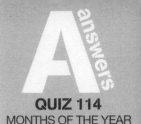

QUESTION 1
Thriller – Michael Jackson
'Billie Jean', 'Rock with You', 'The Girl is Mine'

QUESTION 2
Can't Slow Down – Lionel Richie
'Say You, Say Me', 'Running with the Night', 'Stuck on You'

QUESTION 3
Talk that Talk – Rihanna
'Rude Boy', 'Where Have You Been', 'Birthday Cake'

QUESTION 4
A Date with Elvis – Elvis Presley
'Blue Moon of Kentucky', 'Baby Let's Play House', 'Such a Night'

QUESTION 5
Popped in Souled Out – Wet Wet Wet
'Sweet Little Mystery', 'Sweet Surrender', 'Wishing I was Lucky'

QUESTION 6
Help! – The Beatles
'Drive My Car', 'You've Got to Hide Your Love Away', 'Ticket to Ride'

QUESTION 7
Performance and Cocktails – Stereophonics
'The Bartender and the Thief', 'Local Boy in the Photograph', 'I Wouldn't Believe Your Radio'

QUESTION 8
A Night on the Town – Rod Stewart
'I Don't Want to Talk About It', 'The First Cut is the Deepest', 'Pretty Flamingo'

QUESTION 9
Demon Days – Gorillaz
'Rock the House', 'Dirty Harry', 'Kids with Guns'

QUESTION 10
Sticky Fingers – The Rolling Stones
'Brown Sugar', 'I Got the Blues', 'Tumbling Dice'

QUIZ 114
MONTHS OF THE YEAR

Q1
Kate Bush

Q2
'November Rain'

Q3
'September'

Q4
Brian May

Q5
Bomb the Bass

Q6
Neil Diamond

Q7
'January'

Q8
Jesus and Mary Chain

Q9
October

Q10
'The Calendar Song'

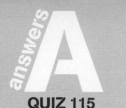

QUIZ 115
NAME THE ALBUM

Q1
Bad – Michael Jackson (1987)

Q2
Employment – Kaiser Chiefs (2005)

Q3
Transformer – Lou Reed (1972; did not chart in UK until 1973)

Q4
Revolver – The Beatles (1966)

Q5
The Great Escape – Blur (1995)

Q6
Love Over Gold – Dire Straits (1982)

Q7
1989 – Taylor Swift (2014)

Q8
Regatta de Blanc – The Police (1979)

Q9
Who's Next – The Who (1971)

Q10
Rockferry – Duffy (2008)

QUIZ 117 POPMASTER
NOT ON TV

QUESTION 1
What was the title of the 2002 debut hit and number one single by the ten-piece vocal group Blazin' Squad?

QUESTION 2
Can you name the Jamaican duo who achieved a top forty hit in 1994 with 'Murder She Wrote'?

QUESTION 3
Which Swedish group made our top twenty in 1993 with a song called 'Wheel of Fortune'?

QUESTION 4
In which 1956 movie did Frank Sinatra and Celeste Holm sing the Cole Porter song 'Who Wants to be a Millionaire'?

QUESTION 5
Which Canadian rock band achieved a top forty hit in 1983 with the double 'A'-sided single 'Countdown' and 'New World Man'?

QUESTION 6
In 1967, which legendary Tamla Motown star achieved his second UK top twenty hit with 'A Place in the Sun'?

QUESTION 7
Which group included a song called 'Match of the Day' on their 1977 hit EP 'Spot the Pigeon'?

QUESTION 8
Can you name the duo who topped the UK chart in 1992 with their recording of 'Would I Lie to You'?

QUESTION 9
In 1978, the Scottish band The Rezillos achieved their one and only UK top forty hit. Can you remember the title?

QUESTION 10
Which group, who scored a number three hit in 1980 with 'Turning Japanese', just missed out on making the top forty with another release later in the same year called 'News at Ten'?

POPMASTER QUIZ 118

NUMBER ONES (1)

In each case, simply name the year these three songs all reached number one

QUESTION 1
'Tiger Feet' by Mud, 'Kung Fu Fighting' by Carl Douglas and 'Gonna Make You a Star' by David Essex

QUESTION 2
'Goodnight Girl' by Wet Wet Wet, 'Deeply Dippy' by Right Said Fred and 'Sleeping Satellite' by Tasmin Archer

QUESTION 3
'Happy' by Pharrell Williams, 'Stay with Me' by Sam Smith and 'Sing' by Ed Sheeran

QUESTION 4
'Heart' by Pet Shop Boys, 'I Owe You Nothing' by Bros and 'He Ain't Heavy, He's My Brother' by The Hollies

QUESTION 5
'King of the Road' by Roger Miller, 'Mr Tambourine Man' by The Byrds and 'Get Off of My Cloud' by The Rolling Stones

QUESTION 6
'Radio' by Robbie Williams, 'Everytime' by Britney Spears and 'Vertigo' by U2

QUESTION 7
'Frozen' by Madonna, 'Deeper Underground' by Jamiroquai and 'It's Like That' by Run-DMC vs Jason Nevins

QUESTION 8
'Return of the Mack' by Mark Morrison, '2 Become 1' by Spice Girls and 'Fastlove' by George Michael

QUESTION 9
'Ghost Town' by The Specials, 'Prince Charming' by Adam & The Ants and 'Being with You' by Smokey Robinson

QUESTION 10
'Space Oddity' by David Bowie, 'Oh Boy' by Mud and 'January' by Pilot

A answers

QUIZ 116
NOT ON THIS ALBUM

Q1
'Rock with You'

Q2
'Say You, Say Me'

Q3
'Rude Boy'

Q4
'Such a Night'

Q5
'Sweet Surrender'

Q6
'Drive My Car'

Q7
'Local Boy in the Photograph'

Q8
'I Don't Want to Talk About It'

Q9
'Rock the House'

Q10
'Tumbling Dice'

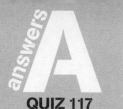

QUIZ 119 POPMASTER
NUMBER ONES (2)

In each case, simply name the year these three songs all reached number one

Q1
'Crossroads'

Q2
Chaka Demus & Pliers

Q3
Ace of Base

Q4
High Society

Q5
Rush

Q6
Stevie Wonder

Q7
Genesis

Q8
Charles & Eddie

Q9
'Top of the Pops'

Q10
The Vapors

QUESTION 1
'The House of the Rising Sun' by The Animals, 'Baby Love' by The Supremes and 'A Hard Day's Night' by The Beatles

QUESTION 2
'Innuendo' by Queen, 'Should I Stay or Should I Go' by The Clash and 'The One and Only' by Chesney Hawkes

QUESTION 3
'No Tomorrow' by Orson, 'America' by Razorlight and 'Patience' by Take That

QUESTION 4
'Everything I Own' by Boy George, 'You Win Again' by the Bee Gees and 'La Bamba' by Los Lobos

QUESTION 5
'Dream Lover' by Bobby Darin, 'Here Comes Summer' by Jerry Keller and 'Roulette' by Russ Conway

QUESTION 6
'So You Win Again' by Hot Chocolate, 'Knowing Me, Knowing You' by ABBA and 'I Feel Love' by Donna Summer

QUESTION 7
'The Power' by Snap!, 'A Little Time' by The Beautiful South and 'World in Motion...' by Englandneworder

QUESTION 8
'Jailhouse Rock' by Elvis Presley, 'Axel F' by Crazy Frog and 'Dakota' by Stereophonics

QUESTION 9
'Sealed with a Kiss' by Jason Donovan, 'Eternal Flame' by The Bangles and 'Swing the Mood' by Jive Bunny and the Mastermixers

QUESTION 10
'Mighty Quinn' by Manfred Mann, 'With a Little Help from My Friends' by Joe Cocker and 'Do it Again' by The Beach Boys

POPMASTER QUIZ 120
NUMBER ONES (3)

In each case, simply name the year these three songs all reached number one

QUESTION 1
'Save Your Kisses for Me' by Brotherhood of Man, 'Don't Go Breaking My Heart' by Elton John & Kiki Dee and 'Under the Moon of Love' by Showaddywaddy

QUESTION 2
'House of Fun' by Madness, 'Beat Surrender' by The Jam and 'Ebony and Ivory' by Paul McCartney with Stevie Wonder

QUESTION 3
'Don't Speak' by No Doubt, 'Beetlebum' by Blur and 'Barbie Girl' by Aqua

QUESTION 4
'Don't Stop Movin'' by S Club 7, 'Can't Get You out of My Head' by Kylie Minogue and 'Uptown Girl' by Westlife

QUESTION 5
'Every Loser Wins' by Nick Berry, 'The Final Countdown' by Europe and 'Don't Leave Me this Way' by The Communards

QUESTION 6
'Someone Like You' by Adele, 'Cannonball' by Little Mix and 'What Makes You Beautiful' by One Direction

QUESTION 7
'Fairground' by Simply Red, 'Some Might Say' by Oasis and 'Earth Song' by Michael Jackson

QUESTION 8
'See My Baby Jive' by Wizzard, 'Rubber Bullets' by 10cc and 'Skweeze Me Pleeze Me' by Slade

QUESTION 9
'Puppet on a String' by Sandie Shaw, 'Silence is Golden' by The Tremeloes and 'Baby Now that I've Found You' by The Foundations

QUESTION 10
'Cars' by Gary Numan, 'Sunday Girl' by Blondie and 'Walking on the Moon' by The Police

Answers

QUIZ 118
NUMBER ONES (1)

Q1
1974

Q2
1992

Q3
2014

Q4
1988

Q5
1965

Q6
2004

Q7
1998

Q8
1996

Q9
1981

Q10
1975

Q1
1964

Q2
1991

Q3
2006

Q4
1987

Q5
1959

Q6
1977

Q7
1990

Q8
2005

Q9
1989

Q10
1968

QUIZ 121 POPMASTER

OFF THE RAK

Questions about the hit record label and its artists

QUESTION 1
Which record producer formed RAK Records in 1969?

QUESTION 2
Name the guitarist with RAK favourites Mud who went on to write number one hits for both Spiller and Kylie Minogue.

QUESTION 3
The singer Clark Datchler released the singles 'I Don't Want You' and 'Things Can't Get Any Worse' on RAK in 1984. They failed to chart, but three years later he reached the Top 10 as lead singer with which group?

QUESTION 4
'Whole Lotta Love' was the first of five Top 40 hits on the label for the band C.C.S. Name one of the other four.

QUESTION 5
What is the first name of Kim Wilde's brother, who both co-wrote her debut hit 'Kids in America' with their father Marty and also produced the song?

QUESTION 6
Having made appearances on *Top of the Pops* dressed as a Womble(!), which guitarist appeared on the show as himself, performing his 1975 hit single 'Motor Bikin''?

QUESTION 7
The American group Exile had its only UK Top 40 hit with which 1978 Top 10 song?

QUESTION 8
Racey's final hit for the label was a 1980 cover version of which early Sixties hit for both Dion and Doug Sheldon?

QUESTION 9
Hot Chocolate had a hit in 1978 with a song that featured in the Don Black/ Geoff Stephens musical *Dear Anyone*, which was about the trials and tribulations of being an agony aunt. What was this Top 20 hit called?

QUESTION 10
Which three-piece group had two hits on the label in the mid-Seventies with the songs 'A Touch Too Much' and 'My Last Night with You'?

POPMASTER QUIZ 122

ON AND OFF

QUESTION 1
Which female singer enjoyed a UK top twenty hit in 2004 with her song 'Call off the Search'?

QUESTION 2
Can you name the soul singer who made the UK top twenty in 1984 with his hit single 'On the Wings of Love'?

QUESTION 3
Which member of The Beatles scored a solo number two hit in 1972 with 'Back off Boogaloo'?

QUESTION 4
What is the title of the 2015 top three hit by Major Lazer and French producer DJ Snake, with vocals by Danish singer MØ?

QUESTION 5
Who achieved a top five album and a top ten single in the Seventies called 'Off the Wall'?

QUESTION 6
Which Sixties UK number one hit by The Rolling Stones featured the song 'Off the Hook' on the 'B' side?

QUESTION 7
Can you name the duo who in 1992 reached number two in the UK with 'On a Ragga trip' and returned to the top forty in 1997 with a re-mixed version?

QUESTION 8
What was the title of the 1997 UK top ten hit single by Propellerheads and David Arnold that shares its title with a James Bond movie?

QUESTION 9
Which member of Madness achieved a solo UK top ten hit in 1995 with the double 'A'-sided hit 'I'm Only Sleeping' and 'Off on Holiday'?

QUESTION 10
In 2014, which recording artist topped the UK chart with his second single, 'Money on My Mind', from his debut album In the Lonely Hour?

Q1
1976

Q2
1982

Q3
1997

Q4
2001

Q5
1986

Q6
2011

Q7
1995

Q8
1973

Q9
1967

Q10
1979

125

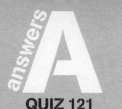

Q1
Mickie Most

Q2
Rob Davis

Q3
Johnny Hates Jazz

Q4
'Walkin'', 'Tap Turns on the Water', 'Brother', 'The Band Played the Boogie'

Q5
Ricky

Q6
Chris Spedding

Q7
'Kiss You All Over'

Q8
'Runaround Sue'

Q9
'I'll Put You Together Again'

Q10
The Arrows

QUIZ 123 POPMASTER
PEACE AND QUIET

QUESTION 1
Which female Icelandic singer achieved a top five hit in 1995 with 'It's Oh So Quiet'?

QUESTION 2
Can you name the Irish trio who achieved a 1966 top three hit in the UK with their cover of Simon & Garfunkel's 'The Sound of Silence'?

QUESTION 3
What was the name of the group whose only UK hit was their 1971 recording of 'Softly Whispering I Love You'?

QUESTION 4
In 1982, what was the title of the hit duet medley between Bing Crosby and David Bowie?

QUESTION 5
What was the name of the group with which John Lennon recorded his 1969 top three hit 'Give Peace a Chance'?

QUESTION 6
What was the title of the hit song that Canadian female singer Sarah McLachlan took into the UK chart in 2000 and again in 2004 with the production duo Delerium?

QUESTION 7
Can you name the group that first made the UK top twenty in 1981 with 'Quiet Life'?

QUESTION 8
After the departure of Brian Poole, what was the title of The Tremeloes' only UK number one hit?

QUESTION 9
What was the title of the 1991 debut top ten hit for Sabrina Johnston?

QUESTION 10
In 1968, New Zealand-born singer John Rowles achieved two UK top twenty hits. The first was 'If I Only Had Time', but what was the title of the second?

POPMASTER QUIZ 124
PICTURE THIS

QUESTION 1
Which Beatle had a Top 10 solo hit in 1973 called 'Photograph'?

QUESTION 2
'Centerfold' was one of two Top 40 UK chart hits by America's J Geils Band. The other was also the title track of their hit album that contained both singles – what is its title?

QUESTION 3
The songs 'Angels', 'Old Before I Die' and 'Let Me Entertain You' all featured on which Robbie Williams album?

QUESTION 4
In 1967, The Who reached the Top 5 singing about 'Pictures of…' who?

QUESTION 5
Which British group released an album and single in 1980 called 'Gentlemen Take Polaroids'?

QUESTION 6
'Kodachrome' is the opening track to which of these solo albums by Paul Simon – Still Crazy After All These Years, There Goes Rhymin' Simon or Paul Simon?

QUESTION 7
Which boy band had a Top 3 hit in 1997 with 'Picture of You'?

QUESTION 8
What type of '…Games' did Lana Del Rey sing about on her 2011 Top 10 debut hit?

QUESTION 9
A song called 'Photograph' was a Top 20 hit in the summer of 2015 for one of the UK's most successful singer-songwriters of recent years. Who is he?

QUESTION 10
The 1982 single 'Wishing (If I Had a Photograph of You)' was the only Top 10 single by A Flock of Seagulls, but the group had three other Top 40 songs. Name one of them.

Q1
Katie Melua

Q2
Jeffrey Osborne

Q3
Ringo Starr

Q4
'Lean On'

Q5
Michael Jackson

Q6
'Little Red Rooster'

Q7
SL2

Q8
'On Her Majesty's Secret Service'

Q9
Suggs

Q10
Sam Smith

answers

QUIZ 123
PEACE AND QUIET

Q1
Björk

Q2
The Bachelors

Q3
The Congregation

Q4
'Peace on Earth - Little Drummer Boy'

Q5
The Plastic Ono Band

Q6
'Silence'

Q7
Japan

Q8
'Silence is Golden'

Q9
'Peace'

Q10
'Hush... Not a Word to Mary'

QUIZ 125 POPMASTER
PROG ROCK

Bands and artists who have been associated with prog rock over the years

QUESTION 1
What are the first names of the trio Emerson, Lake & Palmer?

QUESTION 2
The band East of Eden had its only hit single in 1971 with which Top 10 song?

QUESTION 3
Often considered the UK's first 'concept' album, which group released the 1967 album Days of Future Passed?

QUESTION 4
Despite a run of hit albums, Yes didn't have their first hit single until 1977 with which Top 10 song?

QUESTION 5
Over the course of their chart career, Marillion have had two main lead singers. Name both of them.

QUESTION 6
In 1974, Rick Wakeman had a number one album and won an Ivor Novello award for his live album based on a work by Jules Verne. What was it called?

QUESTION 7
Sonja Kristina is best known as the lead singer with which prog rock group formed in 1970?

QUESTION 8
Which Genesis album includes the songs 'Firth of Fifth', 'The Battle of Epping Forest' and 'I Know What I Like (In Your Wardrobe)'?

QUESTION 9
Over the course of the band's career, which group has released albums called Lizard, Larks' Tongues in Aspic and In the Wake of Poseidon?

QUESTION 10
Featuring vocals by Annie Haslam, the group Renaissance is best remembered for a Top 10 single in 1978 - the band's only hit. What is it called?

POPMASTER QUIZ 126

PSEUDONYMS

These are famous acts who have released records under alternative names

QUESTION 1
Under what name did Ant & Dec achieve a top ten hit in 1994 with 'Let's Get Ready to Rhumble', which went to number one in 2013 when re-released?

QUESTION 2
What was the name of the group who made the top three in 1972 with 'In a Broken Dream', on which Rod Stewart sang the uncredited lead vocals?

QUESTION 3
Under what group name was Eric Clapton featured on the hit single 'Layla?'

QUESTION 4
Prior to achieving hits as Sonny & Cher, under what name did the duo release a couple of singles?

QUESTION 5
The 1968 top ten hit by The Bonzo Dog Doo-Dah Band, 'I'm the Urban Spaceman', was produced by Apollo C Vermouth - a pseudonym for whom?

QUESTION 6
Which member of Queen released a 1973 single version of 'I Can Hear Music' under the name of Larry Lurex?

QUESTION 7
The 1986 debut UK hit by The Bangles, 'Manic Monday', had the composer credit as 'Christopher'. This was a pseudonym for whom?

QUESTION 8
Which American singer and songwriter composed Bobby Vee's 1961 hit 'Rubber Ball' with Aaron Schroeder under his mother's name, Ann Orlowski?

QUESTION 9
Can you name the radio presenter who achieved a northern soul hit in 1978 with his version of Doris Troy's 'I'll do Anything'?

QUESTION 10
Which member of The Beatles wrote the hit 'Badge' for Cream under the name of L'Angelo Misterioso?

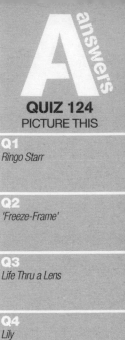

Answers

QUIZ 124
PICTURE THIS

Q1
Ringo Starr

Q2
'Freeze-Frame'

Q3
Life Thru a Lens

Q4
Lily

Q5
Japan

Q6
There Goes Rhymin' Simon

Q7
Boyzone

Q8
'Video Games'

Q9
Ed Sheeran

Q10
*'Space Age Love Song',
'Transfer Affection', 'The More You Live, the More You Love'*

QUIZ 125
PROG ROCK

Q1
Keith Emerson, Greg Lake, Carl Palmer

Q2
'Jig-a-Jig'

Q3
The Moody Blues

Q4
'Wondrous Stories'

Q5
Fish (1981-1988), Steve Hogarth (1989-present)

Q6
Journey to the Centre of the Earth

Q7
Curved Air

Q8
Selling England by the Pound

Q9
King Crimson

Q10
'Northern Lights'

QUIZ 127 POPMASTER
REAL NAMES (1)

Here are the real names of ten successful pop, rap and rock stars. How are they best known?

QUESTION 1
Stefani Joanne Angelina Germanotta

QUESTION 2
David Evans (a guitarist)

QUESTION 3
Stevland Hardaway Judkins

QUESTION 4
Elizabeth Woolridge Grant

QUESTION 5
Gary Webb

QUESTION 6
Ella Marija Lani Yelich-O'Connor

QUESTION 7
Eileen Regina Edwards

QUESTION 8
Georgios Kyriacos Panayiotou

QUESTION 9
Sean Combs

QUESTION 10
Rita Sahatçiu

POPMASTER QUIZ 128
REAL NAMES (2)

Here are the real names of ten successful pop, rap and rock stars. How are they best known?

QUESTION 1
Katheryn Elizabeth Hudson

QUESTION 2
Farrokh Bulsara

QUESTION 3
Tim Bergling

QUESTION 4
Onika Maraj

QUESTION 5
John Simon Ritchie (punk bassist)

QUESTION 6
Tramar Dillard

QUESTION 7
Brian Hugh Warner

QUESTION 8
Anna Mae Bullock

QUESTION 9
John Anthony Gillis

QUESTION 10
Peter Gene Hernandez

Answers

QUIZ 126
PSEUDONYMS

Q1
PJ & Duncan

Q2
Python Lee Jackson

Q3
Derek & The Dominoes

Q4
Caesar & Cleo

Q5
Paul McCartney

Q6
Freddie Mercury

Q7
Prince

Q8
Gene Pitney

Q9
Tony Blackburn

Q10
George Harrison

QUIZ 129 POPMASTER
REFLECTIONS

Q1
Lady Gaga

Q2
The Edge

Q3
Stevie Wonder

Q4
Lana Del Rey

Q5
Gary Numan

Q6
Lorde

Q7
Shania Twain

Q8
George Michael

Q9
Puff Daddy/P. Diddy/Diddy

Q10
Rita Ora

QUESTION 1
Which Motown group achieved a top five hit in 1967 with a song called 'Reflections'?

QUESTION 2
Name the duo consisting of David Van Day and Thereze Bazar who achieved a top five hit in 1981 with 'Mirror Mirror (Mon Amour)'.

QUESTION 3
Can you name the famous rock star who made the top forty in 1994 with 'Objects in the Rear View Mirror May Appear Closer than they Are'?

QUESTION 4
Which successful Motown act achieved a top ten hit in 1972 with 'Lookin' Through the Windows'?

QUESTION 5
Who achieved his debut solo hit in 1978 with the song 'I Love the Sound of Breaking Glass'?

QUESTION 6
After a number of hits with CBS, which Scottish group signed to Decca in 1969, achieving their first hit for the label with 'Reflections of My Life'?

QUESTION 7
Can you name the British group who had their first top forty hit in America and their seventh top ten hit in the UK with 'Look Through Any Window'?

QUESTION 8
Which group reached number two in the UK in 1982 with their hit single 'Mirror Man'?

QUESTION 9
Who topped the American chart and made the UK top five in 1972 with 'I Can See Clearly Now'?

QUESTION 10
Who had a top five hit in 1980 with 'We are Glass'?

POPMASTER **QUIZ 130**
ROCK AND ROLL

QUESTION 1
Can you name the Austrian singer who topped the American chart for three weeks and was number one in the UK for one week with 'Rock Me Amadeus'?

QUESTION 2
Which American group found themselves in the singles chart in 1956 with 'Rockin' Through the Rye'?

QUESTION 3
In 1995, which group scored a major hit with their single 'Roll with It'?

QUESTION 4
'I'm Just a Singer (In a Rock 'n' Roll Band)' was a 1973 top forty hit for which legendary band?

QUESTION 5
Which classic Chuck Berry song became a top ten hit in 1973 for the Electric Light Orchestra?

QUESTION 6
With contributions from the uncredited rappers DMX, Redman and Method Man, which American rock band topped the UK chart for two weeks in 2001 with 'Rollin'?

QUESTION 7
What was the title of the only UK top ten hit for Joan Jett & The Blackhearts that also topped the American chart for seven weeks in 1982?

QUESTION 8
Can you name the group who had their third and final UK top ten hit with 'Roll Away the Stone' in 1973?

QUESTION 9
Which John Fogerty song gave Status Quo a top three hit in 1977?

QUESTION 10
First released in 1973, what was the title of the only hit by Australian-born Kevin Johnson that made the UK chart when re-released in 1975?

Q1
Katy Perry

Q2
Freddie Mercury

Q3
Avicii

Q4
Nicki Minaj

Q5
Sid Vicious

Q6
Flo Rida

Q7
Marilyn Manson

Q8
Tina Turner

Q9
Jack White

Q10
Bruno Mars

QUIZ 131 POPMASTER

ROUGH TRADE

Questions about the influential record label and its artists

Q1
Diana Ross & The Supremes

Q2
Dollar

Q3
Meat Loaf

Q4
The Jackson Five

Q5
Nick Lowe

Q6
Marmalade

Q7
The Hollies

Q8
Human League

Q9
Johnny Nash

Q10
Gary Numan

QUESTION 1
Name the lead singer with Pulp, who released both his 2006 self-titled debut solo album and its 2009 follow-up, Further Complications, on the Rough Trade label.

QUESTION 2
Written by Elvis Costello and Clive Langer, what was the title of Robert Wyatt's 1983 hit single?

QUESTION 3
Which group released the hit albums Meat is Murder and The Queen is Dead on the label in the Eighties?

QUESTION 4
Signed to Fontana Records, the group James first reached the Top 10 in 1991 with a song whose original version was released on Rough Trade in 1989. What is the song?

QUESTION 5
Which band that had hits on Rough Trade in the Noughties with 'Step into My Office Baby' and 'I'm a Cuckoo' took its name from a French TV series of the 1960s?

QUESTION 6
...and what TV series 'appears' to be referenced in the title of The Libertines' 2004 Top 10 hit on the label?

QUESTION 7
Before a run of Top 40 hits on WEA Records, the band formed by singer-songwriter Roddy Frame was signed to Rough Trade for the original releases of the singles 'Oblivious' and 'Walk out to Winter'. Name the band.

QUESTION 8
In 1986, Madness had a hit with a song that had originally been recorded and released on Rough Trade in 1981 by Scritti Politti. What is the song?

QUESTION 9
Rough Trade artists The Sundays wrote and recorded the original version of a song that would become a 1998 Top 10 cover version for Tin Tin Out featuring Shelley Nelson. What is the song?

QUESTION 10
The early UK hits by Canadian band Arcade Fire were all released on Rough Trade. Who is the group's lead singer?

POPMASTER QUIZ 132
ROUND AND AROUND

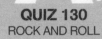

QUIZ 130
ROCK AND ROLL

Q1
Falco

Q2
Bill Haley & His Comets

Q3
Oasis

Q4
The Moody Blues

Q5
'Roll over Beethoven'

Q6
Limp Bizkit

Q7
'I Love Rock 'n' Roll'

Q8
Mott the Hoople

Q9
'Rockin' All Over the World'

Q10
'Rock 'n' Roll (I Gave You the Best Years of My Life)'

QUESTION 1
Which female singer scored top ten hits in the Eighties with 'Set Me Free' and 'Round and Round'?

QUESTION 2
Bing Crosby, Gracie Fields and Ronnie Hilton each released top ten singles in 1957 with their recordings of which song?

QUESTION 3
What was the hit title shared in different songs by East 17 in 1994, Daft Punk in 1997 and ATC in 2002?

QUESTION 4
Can you name the Tamla Motown act that scored a top twenty hit in 1971 with '(Come Round Here) I'm the One You Need' that had first been released in 1966?

QUESTION 5
What was the title of the 1987 top ten hit by Carly Simon that was featured in the movie *Heartburn*?

QUESTION 6
Which American crooner achieved a top ten hit in 1958 with 'Love Makes the World Go Round'?

QUESTION 7
Which group had a top ten hit in 1967 with the title song to the movie *Here We Go Round the Mulberry Bush*?

QUESTION 8
In 2002, which band formed in Newport, Wales, scored a top twenty hit with 'Come Back Around'?

QUESTION 9
Which folk group achieved their only top ten hit in 1975 with 'All Around My Hat'?

QUESTION 10
Can you name the rock band that made their last appearance in the top ten in 1970 with 'Up Around the Bend'?

Q1
Jarvis Cocker (his debut was titled Jarvis)

Q2
'Shipbuilding'

Q3
The Smiths

Q4
'Sit Down'

Q5
Belle and Sebastian

Q6 *The Likely Lads (though 'What Became of the Likely Lads' has nothing to do with Rodney Bewes or James Bolam!)*

Q7
Aztec Camera

Q8
'The Sweetest Girl'

Q9
'Here's Where the Story Ends'

Q10
Win Butler

QUIZ 133 POPMASTER
SECOND TIME AROUND

These are questions about records that were re-issued after their initial outing and became bigger hits second time around

QUESTION 1
Which group first released their single 'Kings of the Wild Frontier' in 1980 to little success, but ended up reaching number two when re-issued a year later?

QUESTION 2
Can you name the American female singer who achieved a minor hit in 1993 with 'Another Sad Love Song' but made the top twenty with it a year later?

QUESTION 3
Which group of brothers who released 'This Ole Heart of Mine' on the Tamla Motown label in 1966 found themselves riding high with the song in 1968?

QUESTION 4
In the year 2000, which group made the top twenty with 'Dancing in the Moonlight', only to find the record climbing into the top ten later the same year when it was re-promoted?

QUESTION 5
What was the title of the Andy Williams hit that first made the top forty in 1967 but found its way into the top ten in 1999 after being featured in a TV commercial for cars?

QUESTION 6
Can you name the group that achieved a top forty hit in 1999 and then a number one in 2000 when their record, 'Don't Call Me Baby', was re-issued?

QUESTION 7
What was the title of the hit record by Freddie Mercury and Montserrat Caballé that first made the top ten in 1987 and then became an even bigger hit in 1992?

QUESTION 8
Which group achieved a top forty hit in 1993 with 'Things Can Only Get Better' but then went to number one when it was re-issued in 1994 and into the Top 20 in 1997 when it was re-issued again following its use in Labour's election campaign?

QUESTION 9
What was the title of the first hit by The Beatles that reached the top twenty in 1962 but climbed into the top five when it was re-issued twenty years later, in 1982?

QUESTION 10
In 1984, The Bluebells reached the top ten with the biggest hit of their career to date, but then went on to top the chart in 1993 when it was re-issued. What was the title of the song?

POPMASTER QUIZ 134

SEE-SAW

QUESTION 1
Which legendary rock band achieved a minor hit in the Sixties with 'Ride My See-Saw'?

QUESTION 2
Can you name the American female singer who made her chart debut in 1972 with the classic song 'The First Time Ever I Saw Your Face'?

QUESTION 3
What was the title of the 1985 top five hit by Dee C Lee that was successfully covered in 2005 by Girls Aloud?

QUESTION 4
Which rock and roll group scored a top ten hit in 1956 with 'See You Later, Alligator'?

QUESTION 5
Can you name the song that John Lennon sang with Elton John on the 1981 live top forty hit duet?

QUESTION 6
Which female singer had a top twenty hit in America and a top forty UK chart entry in 1974 with 'Last Time I Saw Him'?

QUESTION 7
In 1966, which American male and female vocal group made the top twenty with 'I Saw Her Again'?

QUESTION 8
Which larger-than-life American soul singer reached number two in 1976 with 'You See the Trouble with Me'?

QUESTION 9
What was the title of the only top ten hit single of the Sixties by Pink Floyd?

QUESTION 10
Which successful pop group recorded the 1965 top ten hit 'See My Friend'?

Answers

QUIZ 132
ROUND AND AROUND

Q1
Jaki Graham

Q2
'Around the World'

Q3
'Around the World'

Q4
The Miracles

Q5
'Coming Around Again'

Q6
Perry Como

Q7
Traffic

Q8
Feeder

Q9
Steeleye Span

Q10
Creedence Clearwater Revival

137

QUIZ 133
SECOND TIME AROUND

Q1
Adam & The Ants

Q2
Toni Braxton

Q3
The Isley Brothers

Q4
Toploader

Q5
'Music to Watch Girls By'

Q6
Madison Avenue

Q7
'Barcelona'

Q8
D:Ream

Q9
'Love Me Do'

Q10
'Young at Heart'

QUIZ 135 POPMASTER
SHAPES OF THINGS

QUESTION 1
Can you name the vocal group that achieved a top five hit in 1972 with a song called 'Circles'?

QUESTION 2
Which successful American singer and songwriter considered changing his name to Noah Kaminsky early in his career?

QUESTION 3
In 1982, which UK rock band achieved a minor hit with a song titled 'Market Square Heroes'?

QUESTION 4
Can you name the successful American singer who reached our top twenty in 1981 with 'Bermuda Triangle'?

QUESTION 5
On which Coldplay album did the group originally feature the song 'Square One'?

QUESTION 6
Which group reached the UK top five in 2001 with their hit single 'Pyramid Song'?

QUESTION 7
In 2007, which group achieved their 13th top ten hit in the UK with 'The Heart Never Lies'?

QUESTION 8
The song 'Cross My Heart and Hope to Die' appeared in the 1965 movie *Girl Happy*, starring which legendary performer?

QUESTION 9
Which Scottish female singer-songwriter released her fourth album in 2013 with Invisible Empire//Crescent Moon?

QUESTION 10
Can you name the group who achieved their first top ten hit in 1982 with 'Poison Arrow'?

POPMASTER **QUIZ 136**
SINGING COMEDIANS

QUESTION 1
Which Welsh funnyman achieved a top forty hit in 1961 with 'Don't Jump off the Roof Dad'?

QUESTION 2
In 1975, Jasper Carrott achieved a top five hit with a double 'A'-sided single. One of the tracks was called 'Magic Roundabout', but what was the other?

QUESTION 3
Which American comedian made the UK top twenty in 1954 with his parody of The Crew Cuts' hit 'Sh-Boom'?

QUESTION 4
Apart from topping the UK chart in 1971 with 'Ernie (The Fastest Milkman in the West)', Benny Hill achieved two top twenty hits in the Sixties. Can you name either of them?

QUESTION 5
In 1984, Nigel Planer won a BRIT award for 'Best Comedy Record', the only time that category had been included. Under what name did he record his version of Traffic's 'Hole in My Shoe'?

QUESTION 6
None of comedian Des O'Connor's hit records have been intentionally humorous and all of them have made the top thirty, but only one managed to top the UK chart. Can you name it?

QUESTION 7
Which comedy team achieved hits in the Seventies with 'Funky Gibbon', 'Black Pudding Bertha (The Queen of Northern Soul)' and 'Father Christmas Do Not Touch Me'?

QUESTION 8
Recorded live at the Apollo Theatre in Glasgow, which comedian topped the UK chart in 1975 with his parody of Tammy Wynette's hit 'D.I.V.O.R.C.E'?

QUESTION 9
In 1965, Ken Dodd achieved his only UK number one, topping the singles chart for five weeks. What was the title?

QUESTION 10
Which comedian and one-time host of Sunday Night at the London Palladium had a minor hit in 1962 with 'Swinging in the Rain'?

Q1
The Moody Blues

Q2
Roberta Flack

Q3
'See the Day'

Q4
Bill Haley & His Comets

Q5
'I Saw Her Standing There'

Q6
Diana Ross

Q7
The Mamas and The Papas

Q8
Barry White

Q9
'See Emily Play'

Q10
The Kinks

QUIZ 137 POPMASTER
SMOKE GETS IN YOUR EYES

Q1
The New Seekers

Q2
Neil Diamond

Q3
Marillion

Q4
Barry Manilow

Q5
X & Y

Q6
Radiohead

Q7
McFly

Q8
Elvis Presley

Q9
KT Tunstall

Q10
ABC

QUESTION 1
Can you name the group whose only UK top five hit, 'Underwater Love', was featured in a 1997 TV ad for a famous brand of jeans?

QUESTION 2
What was the title of the only UK top forty hit from 1974 by the American rock band Brownsville Station?

QUESTION 3
What hit song has been shared by The Platters in 1959, Blue Haze in 1972, Bryan Ferry in 1974 and John Alford in 1996?

QUESTION 4
What was the title of the UK 1997 top twenty hit by Warren G that also featured Ron Isley?

QUESTION 5
Can you name the Australian female singer who made the UK top ten in 1998 with her hit single 'Smoke'?

QUESTION 6
From 1962, which singer achieved his second top forty UK hit with 'Puff (Up in Smoke)'?

QUESTION 7
Can you name the group who successfully revived The Searchers' 1964 number one hit 'Needles and Pins' in 1977?

QUESTION 8
What was the title of the 2000 top twenty UK hit by DJ Dee Kline that contained a sample of Harry Hill's 'Barking' dialogue from his Channel 4 TV series?

QUESTION 9
First released in 1995, what was the title of the only UK top twenty hit by The Smokin' Mojo Filters?

QUESTION 10
Can you name the group that achieved a UK top ten hit in 2007 with 'Smokers Outside the Hospital Doors'?

POPMASTER QUIZ 138

SOMETHING BEGINNING WITH 'BE'

QUESTION 1
Can you name the actor and singer who reached number two in 1957 with 'Be My Girl'?

Tommy Cooper

QUESTION 2
In 1993, Faith No More achieved a top three hit with a double 'A'-sided single, with one song being 'I'm Easy'. What was the title of the other?

Q2
'Funky Moped'

QUESTION 3
What was the title of the 2003 number one hit by Fatman Scoop featuring The Crooklyn Clan?

Q3
Stan Freberg

QUESTION 4
Can you name the female group produced by Phil Spector who scored their only UK top ten hit in 1963 with 'Be My Baby'?

Q4
'Gather in the Mushrooms',
'Harvest of Love'

QUESTION 5
What hit song title was shared by Lance Fortune in 1960, David Gray in 2003 and Robyn in 2008?

Q5
Neil

QUESTION 6
Which legendary singer from New Orleans scored a top twenty hit in 1959 with 'Be My Guest'?

Q6
'I Pretend'

QUESTION 7
In the late Eighties, Brother Beyond scored three top twenty hits, the first two being 'The Harder I Try' and 'Ain't No Competition'. What was the title of the third?

Q7
The Goodies

QUESTION 8
Can you name the heavy metal band that scored a top three hit in 1992 with 'Be Quick or be Dead'?

Q8
Billy Connolly

QUESTION 9
From 1999, what was the title of the first top ten hit by boy band A1?

Q9
'Tears'

QUESTION 10
Under what collective name did the German duo Gottfried Engels and Ramon Zenker release their 2002 top ten hit 'Be Cool'?

Q10
Norman Vaughan

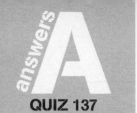

QUIZ 139 POPMASTER
STOP AND GO

QUIZ 137
SMOKE GETS IN YOUR EYES

Q1
Smoke City

Q2
'Smokin' in the Boys' Room'

Q3
'Smoke Gets in Your Eyes'

Q4
'Smokin' Me Out'

Q5
Natalie Imbruglia

Q6
Kenny Lynch

Q7
Smokie

Q8
'I Don't Smoke'

Q9
'Come Together (War Child)'

Q10
Editors

QUESTION 1
Name the group that achieved a UK top three hit in 1966 with 'Stop Stop Stop'.

QUESTION 2
Can you name the group that returned to the chart for the first time in 2000 after a two-year absence with their number one hit 'Go Let it Out'?

QUESTION 3
'Go on Move' was a 1994 top ten UK hit for which act that also featured The Mad Stuntman?

QUESTION 4
Which group made their UK chart debut in 1964 with their number one hit 'Go Now'?

QUESTION 5
What was the title of the 2007 number two hit by Mark Ronson that also featured Daniel Merriweather?

QUESTION 6
In 1997, which female singer successfully revived the Average White Band's 1980 original 'Let's Go Round Again'?

QUESTION 7
Which soul singer first made the chart in 1966 with 'Stop Her on Sight (SOS)' that became a bigger hit when re-issued in 1968?

QUESTION 8
What was the title of the song that topped the UK chart in 2015 by Tinie Tempah, featuring vocals from Jess Glynne?

QUESTION 9
Can you name the group who achieved their only UK top ten hit in 1967 with 'Let's Go to San Francisco'?

QUESTION 10
Which Eighties duo achieved their only major UK hit with their debut chart entry, 'Don't Stop the Music'?

POPMASTER QUIZ 140
STUCK IN THE MIDDLE

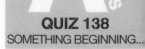
QUESTION 1
Can you name the female group who achieved a top ten hit in 2004 with 'In the Middle'?

QUESTION 2
Which group made their final top forty appearance in 1966 with 'Trouble is My Middle Name'?

QUESTION 3
Which vocal duo made their last top forty appearance in 1963 with 'Trouble is My Middle Name'?

QUESTION 4
In 2001, which female singer made the top five with the revival of Stealers Wheel's 1973 hit 'Stuck in the Middle with You'?

QUESTION 5
Can you name the group that topped the EP chart in 1965 with their four-track release 'The One in the Middle'?

QUESTION 6
What was the name of the group that topped the chart for five weeks in 1971 with 'Chirpy Chirpy Cheep Cheep'?

QUESTION 7
Which duo made the top ten in 2001 with their single 'Up Middle Finger'?

QUESTION 8
Alma Cogan, The Johnston Brothers and Jimmy Parkinson each released hit versions in 1956 of which song?

QUESTION 9
Which boy band achieved a number two hit in 2002 with 'Caught in the Middle'?

QUESTION 10
In 1965, which female singer found herself 'In the Middle of Nowhere'?

Q1
Jim Dale

Q2
'Be Aggressive'

Q3
'Be Faithful'

Q4
The Ronettes

Q5
'Be Mine'

Q6
Fats Domino

Q7
'Be My Twin'

Q8
Iron Maiden

Q9
'Be the First to Believe'

Q10
Paffendorf

143

Q1
The Hollies

Q2
Oasis

Q3
Reel 2 Real

Q4
The Moody Blues

Q5
'Stop Me'

Q6
Louise

Q7
Edwin Starr

Q8
'Not Letting Go'

Q9
The Flowerpot Men

Q10
Yarbrough & Peoples

QUIZ 141 POPMASTER

STUCK ON TWO

This is a round of questions about records that peaked at number two on the UK chart

QUESTION 1
In 1995, Pulp's first record to make the UK top ten was held off the top spot by Robson & Jerome's 'Unchained Melody'/'(There'll be Bluebirds Over) the White Cliffs of Dover'. What was the title?

QUESTION 2
Robson & Jerome's 'I Believe'/'Up on the Roof', also from 1995, managed to keep at bay what many believe was the most iconic single release by Oasis. Can you name it?

QUESTION 3
In 1981 Joe Dolce Music Theatre's 'Shaddup You Face' kept which classic Ultravox record off the top spot for three weeks?

QUESTION 4
Several records lost the chance to top the chart in 1991 thanks to Bryan Adams' 16-week run at number one with '(Everything I Do) I Do it for You'. One such record was the biggest hit achieved by rock band Extreme. Can you name it?

QUESTION 5
Natalie and Nicole were regular visitors to the top of the chart with All Saints but had to settle for number two as Appleton. Which Appleton song did Atomic Kitten trump in 2002 with 'The Tide is High (Get the Feeling)'?

QUESTION 6
For two weeks in 1980, Diana Ross sat at number two with 'Upside Down' whilst which ABBA record refused to give way to this legendary American diva?

QUESTION 7
Status Quo must have been pretty mad when they thought they were about to have their first number one since 1975 with 'What You're Proposing' in 1980, but which Barbra Streisand hit stood in their way for two weeks?

QUESTION 8
Which 1970 single by Free sat at number two for five weeks whilst Mungo Jerry's 'In the Summertime' held fast for four weeks, then, just when they thought it was their turn at the top, Elvis Presley jumped over them with 'The Wonder of You'?

QUESTION 9
Motown Records re-issued 'My Girl' by The Temptations in 1992 due to its appearance in the film of the same name, but it became stuck at number two for two weeks when they were kept off the top spot by which single by Shakespear's Sister?

QUESTION 10
Re-issued from 1969, which iconic David Bowie hit held Roxy Music's 1975 number two 'Love is the Drug' from number one?

POPMASTER QUIZ 142

SUBTITLES

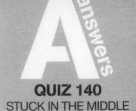

QUIZ 140
STUCK IN THE MIDDLE

QUESTION 1
The T.Rex single 'Get it On' was reduced to being a subtitle on its American release as it was deemed as being too risqué – what was its American title?

QUESTION 2
Tori Amos reached number one in 1997 with a song that has the subtitle '(It's Got to be Big)' – what is it called?

QUESTION 3
What is the subtitle of the Carpenters 1977 hit 'Calling Occupants of Interplanetary Craft'?

QUESTION 4
The Spice Girls re-formed briefly in 2007 and released a Top 20 single called 'Headlines', which had a subtitle that was a lyric from their debut hit 'Wannabe' – what is that subtitle?

QUESTION 5
Which part of Steve Harley and Cockney Rebel's number one 'Make Me Smile Come Up and See Me' is the bit that is officially in brackets?

QUESTION 6
Which David Bowie album contains the hit singles 'Ashes to Ashes', 'Fashion' and 'Up the Hill Backwards'?

QUESTION 7
Bruno Mars reached number one in 2010 with a song that has the subtitle '(Amazing)' – what is it called?

QUESTION 8
Which 1974 single by The Faces has one of the longest ever subtitles of any single release?

QUESTION 9
Human League's first Top 10 hit has the subtitle '(I Believe in Love)' – what is it called?

QUESTION 10
Featured on Abbey Road, what is the subtitle of the Beatles song 'I Want You'?

Q1
Sugababes

Q2
The Four Pennies

Q3
The Brook Brothers

Q4
Louise

Q5
Manfred Mann

Q6
Middle of the Road

Q7
Oxide & Neutrino

Q8
'In the Middle of the House'

Q9
A1

Q10
Dusty Springfield

Q1
'Common People'

Q2
'Wonderwall'

Q3
'Vienna'

Q4
'More than Words'

Q5
'Fantasy'

Q6
'The Winner Takes it All'

Q7
'Woman in Love'

Q8
'All Right Now'

Q9
'Stay'

Q10
'Space Oddity'

QUIZ 143 POPMASTER
THAT'S LIFE

QUESTION 1
From 1998, who made the top three with the hit single 'If You Buy this Record Your Life will be Better'?

QUESTION 2
Can you name the Austrian group whose only major success was the 1985 top ten hit 'Live is Life'?

QUESTION 3
In 2003, which female singer took the song 'Life for Rent' into the top ten?

QUESTION 4
According to their 1971 top twenty hit, which group claimed that 'Life is a Long Song'?

QUESTION 5
Who topped the singles chart for one week in the year 2000 with 'Life is a Rollercoaster'?

QUESTION 6
Can you name the movie that featured the top ten hit duet from the Eighties by Bill Medley and Jennifer Warnes, '(I've Had) the Time of My Life'?

QUESTION 7
Who made their top forty chart debut in 1961 with '(I Wanna) Love My Life Away'?

QUESTION 8
From 1976, can you name the only top ten hit achieved by Sheer Elegance?

QUESTION 9
Which female group made the top three for the third time in 2003 with their third hit, 'Life Got Cold'?

QUESTION 10
From which musical did Nina Simone's 1968 number two hit 'Ain't Got No... I Got Life' originate?

POPMASTER QUIZ 144
THEY'RE ONLY NUMBERS

QUESTION 1
Which one-time milkman from the Isle of Wright made the UK top ten in 1961 with a cover of Gene McDaniels' American hit 'A Hundred Pounds of Clay'?

QUESTION 2
Can you name the successful group that made the UK top ten in 1992 with 'A Million Love Songs'?

QUESTION 3
Which German act topped the UK chart for three weeks with the hit single '99 Red Balloons'?

QUESTION 4
In 1976, which American singer-songwriter found '50 Ways to Leave Your Lover', topping the US chart for three weeks?

QUESTION 5
Can you name the American rap and vocal band that achieved their only UK top ten hit in 1991 with 'Wiggle It'?

QUESTION 6
American actress and singer Connie Stevens achieved a solo hit in 1960. What was the title?

QUESTION 7
'57 Channels (And Nothin' On)' was the claim made in song by which American superstar?

QUESTION 8
Which group topped the American chart for two weeks and enjoyed a top three UK hit in 1970 with 'Mama Told Me Not to Come'?

QUESTION 9
Can you name the psychedelic folk band that released a successful album in 1967 called The 5000 Spirits or the Layers of the Onion?

QUESTION 10
Released in 1988, which female singer achieved the last of eight UK top ten hits with 'Four Letter Word'?

Q1
'Bang a Gong'

Q2
'Professional Widow'

Q3
(The Recognised Anthem of World Contact Day)

Q4
(Friendship Never Ends)

Q5
(Come Up and See Me)

Q6
Scary Monsters (And Super Creeps)

Q7
Just the Way You Are

Q8 'You Can Make Me Dance, Sing or Anything' (Even Take the Dog for a Walk, Mend a Fuse, Fold Away the Ironing Board, or Any Other Domestic Short Comings)

Q9
'Love Action'

Q10
(She's So Heavy)

QUIZ 143
THAT'S LIFE

Q1
The Tamperer featuring Maya

Q2
Opus

Q3
Dido

Q4
Jethro Tull

Q5
Ronan Keating

Q6
Dirty Dancing

Q7
Gene Pitney

Q8
'Life is Too Short Girl'

Q9
Girls Aloud

Q10
Hair

QUIZ 145 POPMASTER
THIS IS NOT MY SONG

Each question lists four songs: one of these songs is not credited to the composer(s) at the start of each question. Do you know which one?

QUESTION 1
Cat Stevens
a) 'Matthew and Son' b) 'The First Cut is the Deepest' c) 'Another Saturday Night' d) 'Lady D'Arbanville'

QUESTION 2
Burt Bacharach & Hal David
a) 'Raindrops Keep Fallin' on My Head' b) 'Make it Easy on Yourself' c) 'What's New Pussycat' d) 'All the Love in the World'

QUESTION 3
John Lennon & Paul McCartney
a) 'Ticket to Ride' b) 'Something' c) 'Hey Jude' d) 'With a Little Help from My Friends'

QUESTION 4
Mick Jagger & Keith Richards
a) 'Jumpin' Jack Flash' b) 'It's All Over Now' c) 'As Tears Go By' d) 'Out of Time'

QUESTION 5
Diane Warren
a) 'Love Don't Cost a Thing' b) 'Only Love Can Hurt Like This' c) 'I Don't Want to Miss a Thing' d) 'How Do I Live'

QUESTION 6
David Bowie
a) 'All the Young Dudes' b) 'The Man Who Sold the World' c) 'Under Pressure' d) 'Sorrow'

QUESTION 7
Prince
a) 'Love... Thy Will be Done' b) 'Nothing Compares 2 U' c) 'Alphabet Street' d) 'Modern Girl'

QUESTION 8
Brian Holland, Lamont Dozier & Eddie Holland
a) 'Reach Out - I'll be There' b) 'You Can't Hurry Love' c) 'The Tears of a Clown' d) 'Heaven Must Have Sent You'

QUESTION 9
Mark Ronson
a) 'Uptown Funk!' b) 'Love is a Losing Game' c) 'Bang Bang Bang' d) 'Slow Down Baby'

QUESTION 10
Jackie De Shannon
a) 'When You Walk in the Room' b) 'Bette Davis Eyes' c) 'Needles and Pins' d) 'Come and Stay with Me'

POPMASTER QUIZ 146
TIME TO PRAY

QUESTION 1
Which American rock band achieved their first UK top twenty hit in 1991 with 'Losing My Religion'?

QUESTION 2
Can you name the legendary American soul singer who achieved UK top five status with her 1968 hit 'I Say a Little Prayer'?

QUESTION 3
Who topped our chart over the first three weeks of December 1999 with his hit single 'The Millennium Prayer'?

QUESTION 4
Which hugely successful vocal group scored their first UK number one in 1993 with a song called 'Pray'?

QUESTION 5
Can you name the singer who topped the singles chart in 1996 with 'Jesus to a Child'?

QUESTION 6
Which Beach Boys UK number two hit single was held off the number one position for two weeks in 1966 by 'Yellow Submarine' and 'Eleanor Rigby' by The Beatles?

QUESTION 7
Which American duo topped the UK chart for four weeks in 1990 with the re-issue of their 1965 top twenty hit 'Unchained Melody'?

QUESTION 8
Which group had two top ten hits in the Nineties with 'International Bright Young Thing' in 1991 and 'The Devil You Know' two years later?

QUESTION 9
In 1983, which successful band sang about the 'Church of the Poison Mind'?

QUESTION 10
Can you name the group that successfully revived The Isley Brothers' 1976 top ten hit 'Harvest for the World' in 1988?

Q1
Craig Douglas

Q2
Take That

Q3
Nena

Q4
Paul Simon

Q5
2 in a Room

Q6
'Sixteen Reasons'

Q7
Bruce Springsteen

Q8
Three Dog Night

Q9
The Incredible String Band

Q10
Kim Wilde

QUIZ 145
THIS IS NOT MY SONG

Q1
'Another Saturday Night'

Q2
'All The Love in the World'

Q3
'Something'

Q4
'It's All Over Now'

Q5
'Love Don't Cost a Thing'

Q6
'Sorrow'

Q7
'Modern Girl'

Q8
'The Tears of a Clown'

Q9
'Love is a Losing Game'

Q10
'Needles and Pins'

QUIZ 147 POPMASTER
TONY VISCONTI

QUESTION 1
The very first number one by T.Rex was a Tony Visconti-produced hit in 1971. What was it called?

QUESTION 2
Tony produced the 1980 album by Hazel O'Connor which was the soundtrack to the film in which she starred. What was the title of both the album and the film?

QUESTION 3
Do it Yourself was the Visconti-produced album by The Seahorses - a group formed by the guitarist from The Stone Roses. Who is he?

QUESTION 4
Adam Ant's final Top 40 hit of the Eighties was a Visconti production with an astronautical theme. What was it called?

QUESTION 5
Often called one of the greatest live albums of the Seventies, which group released the double album Live and Dangerous in 1978?

QUESTION 6
Tony produced the 1975 album by Sparks called Indiscreet, which contained two Top 40 singles. Name either of them.

QUESTION 7
Ringleader of the Tormentors was a 2006 album produced by Tony and recorded by which singer?

QUESTION 8
Who was married to Visconti in the Seventies and sang backing vocals on David Bowie's 'Sound and Vision'?

QUESTION 9
Five of the eight chart hits by Modern Romance in the early Eighties were Visconti productions - 'Cherry Pink and Apple Blossom White' and 'Don't Stop that Crazy Rhythm' were two of them. The other three were all Top 10 hits. Name one of them.

QUESTION 10
Visconti has recently been part of a supergroup that includes Heaven 17's Glenn Gregory, Mick Woodmansey from The Spiders from Mars and Blondie's Clem Burke amongst its members and special guests. What is it called?

POPMASTER QUIZ 148

TOP RANK RECORDS

Top Rank was one of the most successful independent labels of the late Fifties and early Sixties, until it was bought by EMI, who sadly closed it soon afterwards

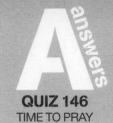

QUESTION 1
Which guitarist achieved a 1959 top ten UK hit with 'Guitar Boogie Shuffle'?

QUESTION 2
The Shirelles' first UK top five hit and American number one from 1961 was released on Top Rank. What was the title?

QUESTION 3
A UK top ten hit for The Hollies in 1963, the original version of 'Stay' topped the American chart in 1961 and reached the UK top twenty, as recorded by which group?

QUESTION 4
Dion's first two UK top twenty hits were released by Top Rank in the early Sixties, the first being 'Runaround Sue'. What was the second?

QUESTION 5
In 1960, Gary Mills made the UK top ten with a song written by Tony Hatch and featured in the movie *Circus of Horrors*. What was the title?

QUESTION 6
The Ventures' debut UK top ten hit was released on Top Rank in 1960. Can you name it?

QUESTION 7
From 1959, can you name the only number one achieved by Craig Douglas - a cover of Sam Cooke's American hit that topped the UK chart for four weeks?

QUESTION 8
Which American rock and roller achieved his only UK top ten hit in 1960 with 'Way Down Yonder in New Orleans'?

QUESTION 9
Which Canadian singer scored his only top twenty UK hit on Top Rank in 1960 with 'What in the World's Come Over You'?

QUESTION 10
Which letters were used as the prefix to Top Rank singles before the actual number: was it CAR, JAR or BAR?

Q1
R.E.M.

Q2
Aretha Franklin

Q3
Cliff Richard

Q4
Take That

Q5
George Michael

Q6
'God Only Knows'

Q7
The Righteous Brothers

Q8
Jesus Jones

Q9
Culture Club

Q10
The Christians

| **Q1** |
| 'Hot Love' |

| **Q2** |
| Breaking Glass |

| **Q3** |
| John Squire |

| **Q4** |
| 'Apollo 9' |

| **Q5** |
| Thin Lizzy |

| **Q6** |
| 'Get in the Swing', 'Looks, Looks, Looks' |

| **Q7** |
| Morrissey |

| **Q8** |
| Mary Hopkin |

| **Q9** |
| 'Best Years of our Lives', 'High Life', 'Walking in the Rain' |

| **Q10** |
| Holy Holy |

QUIZ 149 POPMASTER
TREVOR HORN
Questions about the innovative record producer and his productions

QUESTION 1
For whom did Horn produce the album Slave to the Rhythm?

QUESTION 2
Trevor Horn was a member of The Buggles, who reached number one with 'Video Killed the Radio Star', but they had two other Top 40 hits. Name either of these.

QUESTION 3
Following the demise of The Buggles, Horn became a member of which progressive rock band?

QUESTION 4
What is the title of ABC's number one album that includes the hits 'Poison Arrow', 'The Look of Love' and 'All of My Heart'?

QUESTION 5
What record label was co-founded by Trevor Horn in 1983?

QUESTION 6
What was the first Horn-produced Top 40 hit for the duo Dollar in the Eighties?

QUESTION 7
The 1994 hit 'If I Only Knew' was produced by Horn for which veteran singer?

QUESTION 8
What was the title of Robbie Williams' 2009 album produced by Horn?

QUESTION 9
Trevor produced Rod Stewart's hit cover versions of both 'Tom Traubert's Blues' and 'Downtown Train'. Who wrote these two songs?

QUESTION 10
What nationality are the duo t.A.T.u., who reached number one in 2003 with 'All the Things She Said'?

POPMASTER QUIZ 150

TROJAN RECORDS

Although the Trojan organisation, famous for reggae music, ran several different labels, this quiz concentrates exclusively on releases on the actual imprint

QUESTION 1
Although he achieved a top ten hit in 1972 on the Rhino label with 'Mad About You', what was the title of the only hit by Bruce Ruffin on Trojan from the previous year?

QUESTION 2
From 1974, what was the title of the only hit single released by John Holt?

QUESTION 3
Jamaican reggae group Greyhound achieved three top 20 hits on Trojan but only one made the top ten. Can you name it?

QUESTION 4
Jimmy Cliff achieved a top ten hit on the Island label in 1970 with 'Wild World', but what was the title of his only record to do likewise for Trojan the previous year?

QUESTION 5
'Young, Gifted and Black' by Bob and Marcia was released on the Harry J label and was the first of their two top twenty hits, the second being on Trojan. What was the title?

QUESTION 6
The co-compiler of this quiz book co-produced a 1970 top twenty hit for Trojan titled 'Black Pearl'. Can you name the performer?

QUESTION 7
In 1974, which reggae singer topped the UK chart for three weeks with his revival of the David Gates song 'Everything I Own'?

QUESTION 8
Can you name the group who consisted of members of The Pyramids, who achieved a minor hit in 1980 with 'Skinhead Moonstomp'?

QUESTION 9
What was the title of the only hit by Jamaican singer Nicky Thomas, who made the UK top ten in 1970?

QUESTION 10
From 1971, can you name the only UK top ten hit achieved by The Pioneers?

QUIZ 148
TOP RANK RECORDS

Q1
Bert Weedon

Q2
'Will You Love Me Tomorrow'

Q3
Maurice Williams & The Zodiacs

Q4
'The Wanderer'

Q5
'Look for a Star'

Q6
'Walk Don't Run'

Q7
'Only Sixteen'

Q8
Freddy Cannon

Q9
Jack Scott

Q10
JAR

answers A

QUIZ 149
TREVOR HORN

Q1
Grace Jones

Q2
'The Plastic Age', 'Clean, Clean'

Q3
Yes

Q4
The Lexicon of Love

Q5
ZTT

Q6
'Hand Held in Black and White'

Q7
Tom Jones

Q8
Reality Killed the Video Star

Q9
Tom Waits

Q10
Russian

QUIZ 151 POPMASTER
TWO-HIT WONDERS (1)

These groups or artists had just two Top 40 hits, both of them in the Seventies. Their first was the better known. Can you name the second?

QUESTION 1
Crystal Gayle
'Don't It Make My Brown Eyes Blue' (Top 5 hit in 1977)

QUESTION 2
The Motors
'Airport' (Top 5 hit in 1978)

QUESTION 3
Bachman-Turner Overdrive
'You Ain't Seen Nothing Yet' (Top 3 hit in 1974)

QUESTION 4
Slik
'Forever and Ever' (number 1 in 1976)

QUESTION 5
Plastic Bertrand
'Ça Plane Pour Moi' (Top 10 hit in 1978)

QUESTION 6
Hues Corporation
'Rock the Boat' (Top 10 hit in 1974)

QUESTION 7
Marshall Hain
'Dancing in the City' (Top 3 hit in 1978)

QUESTION 8
Baccara
'Yes Sir I Can Boogie' (number 1 hit in 1977)

QUESTION 9
Dandy Livingstone
'Suzanne Beware of the Devil' (Top 20 hit in 1972)

QUESTION 10
Osibisa
'Sunshine Day' (Top 20 hit in 1976)

POPMASTER QUIZ 152

TWO-HIT WONDERS (2)

These groups or artists had just two Top 40 hits, both of them in the Eighties. Their first was the better known. Can you name the second?

QUESTION 1
Falco
'Rock Me Amadeus' (number 1 in 1986)

QUESTION 2
Landscape
'Einstein a Go-Go' (Top 5 hit in 1981)

QUESTION 3
Sydney Youngblood
'If Only I Could' (Top 3 in 1989)

QUESTION 4
Jim Diamond
'I Should Have Known Better' (number 1 in 1984)

QUESTION 5
Fat Boys
'Wipeout (with the Beach Boys)' (Top 3 hit in 1987)
Their other hit also featured guest artists...

QUESTION 6
Bob Geldof
'This is the World Calling' (Top 30 hit in 1986)

QUESTION 7
Steve Arrington
'Feel So Real' (Top 5 hit in 1985)

QUESTION 8
H2O
'Dream to Sleep' (Top 20 hit in 1983)

QUESTION 9
Robbie Nevil
'C'est la Vie' (Top 3 hit in 1986)

QUESTION 10
Pigbag
'Papa's Got a Brand New Pigbag' (Top 3 hit in 1982)

QUIZ 150
TROJAN RECORDS

Q1
'Rain'

Q2
'Help Me Make it Through the Night'

Q3
'Black and White'

Q4
'Wonderful World, Beautiful People'

Q5
'Pied Piper'

Q6
Horace Faith

Q7
Ken Boothe

Q8
Symarip

Q9
'Love of the Common People'

Q10
'Let Your Yeah be Yeah'

QUIZ 151
TWO-HIT WONDERS (1)

Q1
'Talking in Your Sleep'
(No 11 in '78)

Q2
'Forget About You'
(No 13 in '78)

Q3
'Roll on Down the Highway'
(No 22 in '75)

Q4
'Requiem' (No 24, also in '76)

Q5
'Sha La La La Lee' (No 39,
also in '78)

Q6
'Rockin' Soul' (No 24 in '74)

Q7
'Coming Home' (No 39 in '78)

Q8
'Sorry I'm a Lady' (No 8 in '78)

Q9
'Big City/Think About That'
(No 26 in '73)

Q10
'Dance the Body Music'
(No 31 in '76)

QUIZ 153 POPMASTER
TWO-HIT WONDERS (3)

These groups or artists had just two Top 40 hits in the Nineties and Noughties. Their first was the better known. Can you name the second?

QUESTION 1
Chesney Hawkes
'The One and Only' (number one in 1991)

QUESTION 2
One True Voice
'Sacred Trust'/'After You're Gone' (Top 3 hit in 2002)

QUESTION 3
Maria McKee
'Show Me Heaven' (number one in 1990)

QUESTION 4
Tony Rich Project
'Nobody Knows' (Top 5 hit in 1996)

QUESTION 5
Modjo
'Lady (Hear Me Tonight)' (number one in 2000)

QUESTION 6
Zucchero
'Senza Una Donna (with Paul Young)' (Top 5 hit in 1991)
His other hit was also a duet with another artist...

QUESTION 7
Leon Jackson
'When You Believe' (number 1 in 2007)

QUESTION 8
Adventures of Stevie V
'Dirty Cash' (Top 3 hit in 1990)

QUESTION 9
Sinead Quinn
'I Can't Break Down' (Top 3 hit in 2003)

QUESTION 10
The Mavericks
'Dance the Night Away' (Top 5 hit in 1998)

POPMASTER QUIZ 154
TWO-HIT WONDERS (4)

These groups or artists have had just two Top 40 hits in their careers (as of 2015, that is). Their first was the better known. Can you name the second?

QUESTION 1
Danny Wilson
'Mary's Prayer' (Top 3 hit in 1988)

QUESTION 2
The Toys
'A Lover's Concerto' (Top 5 hit in 1965)

QUESTION 3
Will to Power
'Baby I Love Your Way – Freebird' (Top 10 hit in 1989)

QUESTION 4
Sixpence None the Richer
'Kiss Me' (Top 5 hit in 1999)

QUESTION 5
Doctor & The Medics
'Spirit in the Sky' (number one in 1986)

QUESTION 6
The 5th Dimension
'Aquarius'/'Let the Sunshine In' (Top 20 hit in 1969)

QUESTION 7
Peter Skellern
'You're a Lady' (Top 3 hit in 1972)

QUESTION 8
Patrice Rushen
'Forget Me Nots' (Top 10 hit in 1982)

QUESTION 9
Marti Pellow
'Close to You' (Top 10 in 2001)

QUESTION 10
OC Smith
'The Son of Hickory Holler's Tramp' (Top 3 hit in 1968)

QUIZ 152
TWO-HIT WONDERS (2)

Q1
'Vienna Calling' (No 10, also in '86)

Q2
'Norman Bates' (No 40, also in '81)

Q3
'Sit and Wait' (No 16, also in '89)

Q4
'Hi Ho Silver' (No 5 in '86)

Q5
'The Twist (Yo, Twist)' (with Chubby Checker) ('88 – both songs reached No 2)

Q6
'The Great Song of Indifference' (actually charted higher – No 15 in '90)

Q7
'Dancin' in the Key of Life' (No 21, also in '85)

Q8
'Just Outside of Heaven' (No 38 also in '83)

Q9
'Dominoes' (No 26 in '87)

Q10
'The Big Bean' (No 40, also in '82)

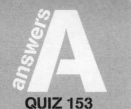

QUIZ 155 POPMASTER
UK TOUR (1)

Q1
'I'm a Man Not a Boy' (No 27, also in '91)

QUESTION 1
Which group had both a hit single and album in 1979 called 'London Calling'?

Q2
'Shakespeare's Way with Words' (No 10 in '03)

QUESTION 2
Mick Jones of The Clash and Big Audio Dynamite guested on a 1990 Top 20 single by Aztec Camera. What was it called?

Q3
'I'm Gonna Soothe You' (No 35 in '93)

QUESTION 3
Which group sang about 'Winchester Cathedral' on their 1966 Top 5 debut hit?

Q4
'Like a Woman' (No 27, also in '96)

QUESTION 4
The roots of the groups Heaven 17, Human League, Arctic Monkeys, ABC and Pulp are all in which South Yorkshire city?

Q5
'Chillin" (No 12 in '01)

QUESTION 5
The singles 'Sour Times' and 'Glory Box' both feature on the 1994 double-platinum album Dummy, recorded by a band who take their name from a town on the Severn Estuary. What is their name?

Q6
'Miserere' (with Luciano Pavarotti) (No 15 in '92)

QUESTION 6
Where were Fiddler's Dram heading on their 'Daytrip', according to the title of their 1979 Top 3 single?

Q7
'Don't Call this Love' (No 3 in 2008)

QUESTION 7
Which footballer was billed alongside Lindisfarne on the 1990 Top 3 hit 'Fog on the Tyne (Revisited)'?

Q8
'Body Language' (No 29, also in '90)

QUESTION 8
What is the location of the 'Airport' Cats U.K. sang about on their only Top 40 hit in the late Seventies?

Q9
'What You Need Is...' (No 19 in 2003)

QUESTION 9
'Sunshine on Leith' was the title of a 1988 single by which duo?

Q10
'I've Got this Feeling' (No 27, also in '98)

QUESTION 10
What was the title of the sixth and final Top 10 hit for Gerry & The Pacemakers in the Sixties?

POPMASTER QUIZ 156
UK TOUR (2)

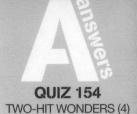

QUIZ 154
TWO-HIT WONDERS (4)

QUESTION 1
The 1966 Simon & Garfunkel album Parsley, Sage, Rosemary & Thyme opens with the duo's version of which traditional English ballad?

QUESTION 2
Which group sang 'Come to Milton Keynes' in 1985?

QUESTION 3
What type of 'Dagger' did The Fratellis sing about on their 2006 Top 5 hit?

QUESTION 4
The 1991 Top 10 single 'It's Grim Up North' was the only hit for a duo that also recorded as The KLF and The Timelords, but how were they billed on this hit?

QUESTION 5
Although it missed out on being a Top 40 hit, which Kent seaside town was the destination for a Chas and Dave single in 1982?

QUESTION 6
Which American group released the 1986 single 'Going Down to Liverpool'?

QUESTION 7
Where did the 'Cowboy' come from that Mike Harding sang about on his 1975 hit?

QUESTION 8
Which group released their Top 3 debut album London 0 Hull 4 in 1986?

QUESTION 9
The Wings number one 'Mull of Kintyre' was a double 'A' side with which other song?

QUESTION 10
Which easy listening singer and whistler was going to leave 'Durham Town' in 1969?

Q1
'The Second Summer of Love'
(No 23, also in '88)

Q2
'Attack' (No 36 in '66)

Q3
'I'm Not in Love' (10cc cover)
(No 29 in '90)

Q4
'There She Goes' (La's cover)
(No 14 in '99)

Q5
'Burn' (No 29, also in '86)

Q6
'Wedding Bell Blues' (No 16
in '70)

Q7
'Hold on to Love' (No 14 in '75)

Q8
'I was Tired of Being Alone'
(No 39 ,also in '82)

Q9
I've Been Around the World
(No 28, also in '01)

Q10
Together (No 25 in '77)

QUIZ 155
UK TOUR (1)

Q1
The Clash

Q2
'Good Morning Britain'

Q3
The New Vaudeville Band

Q4
Sheffield

Q5
Portishead

Q6
Bangor - 'Daytrip to Bangor (Didn't We Have a Lovely Time)'

Q7
Paul Gascoigne (billed as Gazza and Lindisfarne)

Q8
'Luton Airport'

Q9
The Proclaimers (just missed Top 40 - it stalled at No.41)

Q10
'Ferry 'Cross the Mersey'

QUIZ 157 POPMASTER
UPS AND DOWNS

QUESTION 1
What hit song title was shared by Matt Willis in 2006 and Take That in 2009?

QUESTION 2
Can you name the act in which Jim Diamond was a member and achieved just one UK hit in 1982 with 'I Won't Let You Down'?

QUESTION 3
Which legendary soul group scored a UK top ten hit in 1974 with 'Down on the Beach Tonight'?

QUESTION 4
Can you name the male trio who scored a 2009 top ten hit in the UK with 'Uprising'?

QUESTION 5
In 1970, which female Tamla Motown act scored a top ten hit with 'Up the Ladder to the Roof'?

QUESTION 6
'Uptown Funk!' was a 2015 UK number one hit for Mark Ronson that featured which other successful performer?

QUESTION 7
What was the title of the 1999 UK top ten hit by Tom Jones and The Cardigans?

QUESTION 8
Which one-time lead singer of the group Pickettywitch achieved an American top twenty hit in 1975 with 'Up in a Puff of Smoke', co-written and produced by the co-author of this quiz book, Phil Swern?

QUESTION 9
Which successful group topped the UK chart in 2015 with 'Drag Me Down'?

QUESTION 10
Can you name the group whose only UK hit was with the 1978 top ten hit 'Breaking Up Again'?

POPMASTER QUIZ 158
WAS IT SOMETHING I SAID?

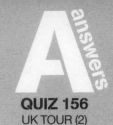

QUESTION 1
Barry White asks for "One ticket please…" in the introduction to which of his Top 10 hits?

QUESTION 2
What is the name of Beyoncé's husband, who raps on her number one hit 'Crazy in Love'?

QUESTION 3
On which Rolling Stones single does Mick Jagger say he'll be your "knight in shining armour"?

QUESTION 4
Who asks if we all "wanna go down the Devil Gate Drive" at the beginning of her 1974 number one?

QUESTION 5
On which Frankie Goes to Hollywood number one does Holly Johnson want to "protect you from the hooded claw"?

QUESTION 6
The song 'Have You Seen Her' begins with a long spoken section and was a Top 5 hit in both 1972 and 1975 for which American vocal group?

QUESTION 7
Florence + The Machine had a Top 3 hit in 2010 with a live single that featured a rap by Dizzee Rascal. What was it called?

QUESTION 8
At the start of 'Ballroom Blitz' by The Sweet, singer Brian Connolly asks the three other band members if they're ready. What are their names?

QUESTION 9
Which actor recites the verses on the song 'Parklife', by Blur?

QUESTION 10
On which of Blondie's hit singles does Debbie Harry talk about "Fab Five Freddie", "eatin' cars" and a "man from Mars"?

Q1
'Scarborough Fair' (their version is actually called 'Scarborough Fair/Canticle')

Q2
The Style Council

Q3
'Chelsea Dagger'

Q4
Justified Ancients of Mu Mu

Q5
'Margate' (it reached No.46)

Q6
The Bangles (it reached No.56)

Q7
Rochdale

Q8
The Housemartins

Q9
'Girls' School'

Q10
Roger Whittaker

QUIZ 157
UPS AND DOWNS

Q1
'Up All Night'

Q2
PhD

Q3
The Drifters

Q4
Muse

Q5
The Supremes

Q6
Bruno Mars

Q7
'Burning Down the House'

Q8
Polly Brown

Q9
One Direction

Q10
Goldie

QUIZ 159 POPMASTER
WATER OR WINE

QUESTION 1
Which legendary singer and actor achieved an American top forty hit in 1967 with 'Little Ole Wine Drinker Me'?

QUESTION 2
In 1957, Tommy Steele had a top five UK success with the double 'A'-sided single 'A Handful of Songs' and which other song?

QUESTION 3
What title is shared by different hit songs from Paul McCartney in 1980 and TLC in 1995, both of which made the UK top ten?

QUESTION 4
Under what name is American singer-songwriter Samuel 'Sam' Beam better known?

QUESTION 5
Which American rock band took the song 'Black Water' to the top of the US chart in 1974?

QUESTION 6
Best known for her hit single 'The Clapping Song', which female singer recorded the 1966 novelty song 'Ever See a Diver Kiss His Wife While the Bubbles Bounce About Above the Water'?

QUESTION 7
Originally released in 1966, which act achieved a UK top forty hit in 1972 with the instrumental 'Wade in the Water'?

QUESTION 8
In 1968, which Neil Diamond song gave Jimmy James & The Vagabonds their first top forty hit?

QUESTION 9
Can you name the female singer who took a glass of 'Lilac Wine' into the UK top twenty in 1978?

QUESTION 10
First released in 1985 then re-issued in 1991, what was the title of the only top ten hit achieved by The Waterboys?

POPMASTER QUIZ 160

WITH IMMEDIATE EFFECT

These are questions about the short-lived yet very successful Sixties record label Immediate, set up by record producer Andrew Oldham

QUESTION 1
P.P. Arnold achieved two top forty hits on Immediate. The biggest was 'The First Cut is the Deepest', but what was the title of the second?

QUESTION 2
Who wrote Chris Farlowe's 1966 number one hit 'Out of Time'?

QUESTION 3
After leaving Decca in 1966, what was the title of the first top twenty hit for The Small Faces on Immediate the following year?

QUESTION 4
Can you name the group that went on to achieve hits with 'Happy Together' and 'She'd Rather be with Me' who released just one single on Immediate, 'You Baby'?

QUESTION 5
Vocal duo Dave Skinner and Andrew Rose achieved a top forty hit in 1966 with 'Sittin' on a Fence'. Under what collective name did they release their single?

QUESTION 6
In 1969, Fleetwood Mac reached number two in the singles chart with their only hit on Immediate. What was the title?

QUESTION 7
Which group topped the chart in 1969 for two weeks with '(If Paradise Is) Half as Nice'?

QUESTION 8
Can you name the American number one from 1965 by The McCoys that made the UK top five when released on Immediate?

QUESTION 9
What was the name of the group formed by Steve Marriott and Peter Frampton that made the top five in 1969 with 'Natural Born Bugie'?

QUESTION 10
Which rock band saw their arrangement of 'America' from *West Side Story* make the top forty in 1968?

QUIZ 158
WAS IT SOMETHING I SAID

Q1
'Let the Music Play'

Q2
Jay Z

Q3
'Emotional Rescue'

Q4
Suzi Quatro

Q5
'The Power of Love'

Q6
The Chi-Lites

Q7
'You Got the Dirtee Love' (a version of The Source/Candi Staton hit 'You Got the Love')

Q8
Steve (Priest), Andy (Scott) and Mick (Tucker)

Q9
Phil Daniels

Q10
'Rapture'

QUIZ 159
WATER OR WINE

Q1
Dean Martin

Q2
'Water Water'

Q3
'Waterfalls'

Q4
Iron & Wine

Q5
The Doobie Brothers

Q6
Shirley Ellis

Q7
The Ramsey Lewis Trio

Q8
'Red Red Wine'

Q9
Elkie Brooks

Q10
'The Whole of the Moon'

QUIZ 161 POPMASTER
CHAMPION OF CHAMPIONS (1)

These are the toughest questions you'll ever face on PopMaster – reserved for the champions who come back for our special winners' shows

QUESTION 1
The band The Members had its only two Top 40 singles in 1979. 'The Sound of the Suburbs' was one, what was the other?

QUESTION 2
Which one-time *Home and Away* actress had hits in 1997 called 'Everything I Wanted' and 'All I Wanna Do'?

QUESTION 3
What is the name of the English art design group that designed album sleeves in the Seventies for 10cc, Pink Floyd, Peter Gabriel and Led Zeppelin, amongst others?

QUESTION 4
'My Boy Lollipop' was a Top 3 hit for Millie in 1964, but she released another single that year which was to be her only other Top 40 hit. What is it called?

QUESTION 5
Which group's only Top 40 hit was in 1994 with the Top 3 song 'Compliments on Your Kiss'?

QUESTION 6
Which two film stars had a hit in 2001 with the song 'Come What May'?

QUESTION 7
The duo Baccara may come from Spain, but which country did they represent at the 1978 Eurovision Song Contest?

QUESTION 8
David Hasselhoff's 2006 Top 10 hit 'Jump in My Car' was a cover of a song originally recorded in 1975 by an Australian-based rock band. What were they called?

QUESTION 9
Which two David Bowie singles in the Nineties either musically or lyrically reference his song 'Space Oddity'?

QUESTION 10
M is often considered a one-hit wonder for the 1979 Top 3 hit 'Pop Muzik', which also reached the Top 20 ten years later as a remix. But there was one other Top 40 hit for the group. What was it called?

POPMASTER QUIZ 162

CHAMPION OF CHAMPIONS (2)

Really tough stuff – have you got what it takes?

QUESTION 1
Following hits in the Seventies as the Tom Robinson Band, Tom Robinson had two further Top 40 solo hits in the Eighties. Name both of them.

Q1
'Angel of the Morning'

QUESTION 2
Which one-time Coronation Street actor had Top 40 hits in 1998 with the songs 'The Heart's Lone Desire' and a version of the Hall & Oates song 'She's Gone', which featured Destiny's Child as guest artists?

Q2
Mick Jagger and Keith Richards

QUESTION 3
The band The Merton Parkas had its only Top 40 hit in 1979. What was it called?

Q3
'Here Comes the Nice'

QUESTION 4
Prior to her radio and television career, Lauren Laverne reached the charts in the Nineties as the lead singer with which group?

Q4
The Turtles

QUESTION 5
Jess Glynne featured on Clean Bandit's number one 'Rather Be' in 2014, but she also featured on another number one that year – a song called 'My Love'. Who recorded this?

Q5
Twice as Much

QUESTION 6
Peter Blake designed the cover of Sgt. Pepper's Lonely Hearts Club Band, but who designed the drum skin in the centre of the sleeve?

Q6
'Man of the World'

QUESTION 7
...and which 1995 number one album by Paul Weller has a sleeve designed by Peter Blake?

Q7
Amen Corner

QUESTION 8
What links the Elvis Presley number ones 'All Shook Up', 'It's Now or Never' and 'The Wonder of You'?

Q8
'Hang on Sloopy'

QUESTION 9
Which Jackson brother left and which Jackson joined when The Jackson 5 changed record labels in the mid-Seventies and became The Jacksons?

Q9
Humble Pie

QUESTION 10
The group Liquid Gold had all three of its Top 40 hits in 1980 – both 'Dance Yourself Dizzy' and 'Substitute' reached the Top 10, but the third languished at No.32. What was it called?

Q10
The Nice

Q1
'Offshore Banking Business'

Q2
Dannii Minogue

Q3
Hipgnosis

Q4
'Sweet William'

Q5
Red Dragon (full title Red Dragon with Brian and Tony Gold)

Q6
Nicole Kidman and Ewan McGregor (from the film Moulin Rouge)

Q7
Luxembourg

Q8 Ted Mulry Gang (lead singer Mulry wrote it and it spent 6 weeks as Australian No.1 in 1976)

Q9 'Hallo Spaceboy' ("Ground to Major, bye bye Tom"), 'Buddha of Suburbia' (a 'Space Oddity' chord sequence)

Q10
'Moonlight and Muzak' (peaked at No 33 in January '80)

QUIZ 163 POPMASTER
CHAMPION OF CHAMPIONS (3)
Really tough stuff – have you got what it takes?

QUESTION 1
Name the British group that had its only chart hits in 1971 with the Top 20 song 'Tomorrow Night' and the Top 5 single 'Devil's Answer'.

QUESTION 2
What comes next in this sequence – Faith, Listen Without Prejudice Volume 1, Older, Songs from the Last Century... ?

QUESTION 3
Released in 1976, what is the title of Twiggy's one and only Top 40 appearance?

QUESTION 4
In which year were these three songs all American number ones? 'Love is Here and Now You're Gone' by The Supremes, 'Happy Together' by The Turtles and 'Windy' by The Association.

QUESTION 5
When Kym Marsh left the *Popstars* group Hear'Say, she was replaced by a male singer. What was he called?

QUESTION 6
The Britpop-era band Menswear had three Top 20 and two further Top 30 singles in the mid-Nineties. Name one of these five hits.

QUESTION 7
Complete this band line-up: Noddy Holder, Dave Hill, Jim Lea and who?

QUESTION 8
Of the nine songs on the original release of Michael Jackson's album Thriller, six of them were released as singles in the UK – only three were not. Name one of these three songs.

QUESTION 9
Who produced The Special AKA's 1984 single 'Nelson Mandela'?

QUESTION 10
What one-word song title has provided different hits for Earth Wind & Fire, Mariah Carey and Appleton?

POPMASTER QUIZ 164

CHAMPION OF CHAMPIONS (4)

Really tough stuff – have you got what it takes?

QUESTION 1
Released in 1978, what is the title of the only hit single by Mike Oldfield's sister, Sally Oldfield?

QUESTION 2
In 1994, which group spent 14 weeks at number one in America with 'I'll Make Love to You', then knocked themselves off the top of the chart with their follow-up, 'On Bended Knee', which spent six weeks at number one?

QUESTION 3
What is the title of Meghan Trainor's 2015 number one album?

QUESTION 4
Released in 1981, the group whose only Top 40 hit was 'Me and Mr Sanchez' was called Blue... what?

QUESTION 5
Madonna had over 50 chart hits in the 20th century, but only four of these failed to reach the Top 10. name one of these four songs.

QUESTION 6
Although they are not related, what are the first names of the three members of the original hit line-up of Duran Duran with the surname Taylor?

QUESTION 7
Which Carole King song was a hit for the singer Martika in 1989?

QUESTION 8
Which American group reached the singles chart in 1975 with '7-6-5-4-3-2-1 (Blow Your Whistle)'?

QUESTION 9
Which Rolling Stones LP from the Sixties begins with 'Gimme Shelter' on side one and ends side two with 'You Can't Always Get What You Want'?

QUESTION 10
After TV's *Popstars: The Rivals*, four girls who didn't make it into Girls Aloud and five boys who didn't make it into One True Voice both formed groups and both had Top 40 hits. Name both the girl group and the boy band.

QUIZ 163
CHAMPIONS (3)

Q1
Atomic Rooster

Q2
Patience (studio albums by George Michael)

Q3
'Here I Go Again'

Q4
1967

Q5
Johnny Shentall (married to Lisa Scott-Lee of Steps)

Q6
'Daydreamer', 'Stardust', 'Sleeping In', 'Being Brave', 'We Love You'

Q7
Don Powell (Slade)

Q8 *'Baby be Mine', 'Human Nature', 'The Lady in My Life' (Human Nature was released as a single in the USA)*

Q9
Elvis Costello

Q10
'Fantasy'

QUIZ 165 POPMASTER

CHAMPION OF CHAMPIONS (5)

Really tough stuff – have you got what it takes?

QUESTION 1
Which Pink Floyd studio album was released after Wish You Were Here but before The Wall?

QUESTION 2
What is the name of the singer who regularly appeared in the TV series *Ally McBeal* and what is the title of her 1998 debut Top 10 single?

QUESTION 3
Who is the drummer in Coldplay?

QUESTION 4
Released in late 1978, what is both the title and subtitle of the only Top 10 hit for the American singer Paul Evans?

QUESTION 5
'Sleepwalk' was the title of the 1980 Top 40 debut by which group?

QUESTION 6
David Bowie's son, once known as Zowie, is now a successful director of the films *Moon* and *Source Code*. What is he called?

QUESTION 7
The 1992 Top 5 single 'Just Another Day' was the biggest hit for the Cuban-born singer Jon Secada, but he had four other Top 40 hits that decade. Name one of them.

QUESTION 8
The song 'I Want an Alien for Christmas' was a Top 40 hit in 1997 for which American group?

QUESTION 9
Bourgeois Tagg had its only chart hit in 1988 – what was it called?

QUESTION 10
Which record label released all the hits in the 1990s by The Beautiful South, as well as several singles by Paul Weller and Billy Bragg?

POPMASTER **QUIZ 166**

CHAMPION OF CHAMPIONS (6)

Really tough stuff – have you got what it takes?

QUIZ 164
CHAMPIONS (4)

QUESTION 1
What was the title of Dexy's Midnight Runners' 1986 hit theme song to the TV show *Brush Strokes*?

Q1
'Mirrors'

QUESTION 2
Who was the drummer with Joy Division and is the drummer with New Order?

Q2
Boyz II Men

QUESTION 3
Which record label released all the hits in the 1990s by Blur, as well as several singles by Jesus Jones and Shampoo?

Q3
Title

QUESTION 4
In 1973, Mud had three hit singles – their debut hit 'Crazy' and their first Top 10 with 'Dyna-mite', but which single was sandwiched between these two?

Q4
Blue Rondo a la Turk

QUESTION 5
What are the surnames of the original hit five-piece line-up of Boyzone?

Q5 *'Lucky Star' (No.14 in '84), 'Take a Bow' (No.16 in '94), 'Oh Father', 'One More Chance' (No.1 and No.11, both in '96)*

QUESTION 6
Who was the lyricist of Elton John's hits 'Blue Eyes', 'Part Time Love' and 'Little Jeannie'?

Q6
John, Roger, Andy

QUESTION 7
What comes next in this sequence – Generation Terrorists, Gold Against the Soul, The Holy Bible... ?

Q7
'I Feel the Earth Move'

QUESTION 8
Which singer's only Top 40 hit was in 1984 with the song 'Bird of Paradise'?

Q8
The Rimshots

QUESTION 9
Released in 1975, which of Showaddywaddy's singles was the group's first hit cover version rather than a self-penned song?

Q9
Let It Bleed

QUESTION 10
Which actress had a Top 10 single in 2001 called 'What If'?

Q10
Clea, Phixx

QUIZ 165
CHAMPIONS (5)

Q1
Animals

Q2
*Vonda Shepard, 'Searchin'
My Soul'*

Q3
Will Champion

Q4
*'Hello, This is Joannie (The
Telephone Answering Machine
Song)'*

Q5
Ultravox

Q6
Duncan Jones

Q7
*'Do You Believe in Us', 'Angel',
'Do You Really Want Me', 'If
You Go'*

Q8
Fountains of Wayne

Q9
'I Don't Mind at All'

Q10
Go! Discs

QUIZ 167 POPMASTER
CHAMPION OF CHAMPIONS (7)
Really tough stuff – have you got what it takes?

QUESTION 1
Which group released albums in the Eighties called Argy Bargy, East Side
Story and Cosi Fan Tutti Frutti?

QUESTION 2
The production duo Shut Up and Dance, aided by singer Peter Bouncer,
completely reworked Marc Cohn's 'Walking in Memphis' into a 1992 Top 3
dance track, complete with new lyrics. What was this version called?

QUESTION 3
Which Turkish-born producer worked on the Average White Band's 'Pick Up
the Pieces', the Bee Gees' 'Jive Talkin'', Chaka Khan's 'I Feel for You', 'Waiting
for a Star to Fall' by Boy Meets Girl and 'Against All Odds' by Phil Collins?

QUESTION 4
Taylor Swift made her debut on the albums chart in 2009 with which Top
5 hit?

QUESTION 5
Which UK group featuring singer Roger Chapman made its chart debut in
1969 with 'No Mule's Fool' and had hits in the early Seventies with 'Strange
Band', 'Burlesque' and the Top 10 song 'In My Own Time'?

QUESTION 6
Tasmin Archer is often considered a one-hit wonder for her 1992 number
one 'Sleeping Satellite', but she had four other Top 40 hits that decade.
Name one of them.

QUESTION 7
After he left the band Razorlight, drummer Andy Burrows began playing with
an existing American band and also formed his own new group. Name either
of these bands.

QUESTION 8
What comes next in this sequence: Sigh No More by Mumford & Sons, 21
by Adele, Our Version of Events by Emeli Sandé, AM by Arctic Monkeys... ?

QUESTION 9
Which British group had all three of its Top 40 hits in 1964 with the songs
'Tell Me When', 'Like Dreamers Do' and 'Three Little Words (I Love You)'?

QUESTION 10
Who is the lyricist of the James Bond theme songs 'The World is Not
Enough', 'Diamonds Are Forever' and 'Thunderball'?

POPMASTER QUIZ 168

CHAMPION OF CHAMPIONS (8)
Really tough stuff – have you got what it takes?

QUESTION 1
Prior to his solo career, Ricky Martin had been a member of which Puerto Rican boy band?

QUESTION 2
What are the first names of the Motown writing and production team Holland-Dozier-Holland?

QUESTION 3
At the time of publication of this book, what do all 12 of the Pet Shop Boys' studio albums have in common – apart from being written and recorded by the duo?!

QUESTION 4
What is the title of the 1978 Top 30 hit recorded by Paper Lace with the Nottingham Forest football team?

QUESTION 5
Who comes next in this sequence: Jessie J, Jessie J, Kylie Minogue, Rita Ora... ?

QUESTION 6
The singer Alex Parks, who won the second series of *Fame Academy*, went on to have two hit singles. Name either of them.

QUESTION 7
Which two groups combined forces to release the 2015 eponymously titled Top 20 album FFS?

QUESTION 8
What was the title of the 1986 hit by Meat Loaf featuring John Parr?

QUESTION 9
Released in 1975 and 1977, the songs 'Save Me' and 'Everybody's Talkin' 'bout Love' were the first and last Top 40 hits for which female vocal group?

QUESTION 10
Eminem's 1999 Top 3 debut hit 'My Name Is' features a sample from which song written and recorded by Labi Siffre?

Q1
'Because of You'

Q2
Stephen Morris

Q3
Food Records

Q4
'Hypnosis'

Q5
Keating, Lynch, Duffy, Graham, Gateley (Ronan, Shane, Keith, Mikey, Stephen)

Q6
Gary Osborne

Q7
Everything Must Go (studio albums by Manic Street Preachers)

Q8
Snowy White (released Dec '83, entered the Top 40 early '84)

Q9
'Three Steps to Heaven'

Q10
Kate Winslet

Q1
Squeeze

Q2
'Raving I'm Raving'

Q3
Arif Mardin

Q4
Fearless

Q5
Family

Q6
'In Your Care', 'Lords of the New Church', 'Arienne', 'Shipbuilding'

Q7
We Are Scientists (US band), I Am Arrows (his new group)

Q8
x by Ed Sheeran (winners of 'Album of the Year' at the BRIT Awards from 2011 to 2015)

Q9
The Applejacks

Q10
Don Black

QUIZ 169 POPMASTER
CHAMPION OF CHAMPIONS (9)

Really tough stuff – have you got what it takes?

QUESTION 1
Russell Thompkins Jr was the lead singer on a run of hits in the Seventies for which American vocal group?

QUESTION 2
The British singer-songwriter Amy Studt had her only two Top 10 hits in 2003 from her album False Smiles. Name either of these songs.

QUESTION 3
Released in 1964, what was the first Bob Dylan studio album not to feature his name in its title?

QUESTION 4
Who was the brains behind the late Eighties/early Nineties dance group S-Express?

QUESTION 5
What is the title of the 1975 compilation album of songs by John Lennon and the Plastic Ono Band?

QUESTION 6
Which group had Top 10 hits in the Nineties with 'Perseverance', 'Bad Actress' and 'Tequila'?

QUESTION 7
The singer Jackie Lee had her only two chart hits in 1968 and 1971. The first was billed as 'Jacky', but both were theme songs to TV programmes. Name both songs.

QUESTION 8
In which year were these three songs all American number ones: 'You Needed Me' by Anne Murray, 'Shadow Dancing' by Andy Gibb and 'Hot Child in the City' by Nick Gilder?

QUESTION 9
What is the title of the 2013 number one album by John Newman that includes the number one single 'Love Me Again' and the Top 10 hit 'Cheating'?

QUESTION 10
Having recorded three of the most enduring rock 'n' roll hits of the Fifties, who also had Top 10 hits that decade with 'Rock-a-Beatin' Boogie', 'The Saints Rock 'N Roll' and 'Don't Knock the Rock'?

POPMASTER QUIZ 170

CHAMPION OF CHAMPIONS (10)
Really tough stuff – have you got what it takes?

QUESTION 1
What are the full names (first and surname) of the three members of the Thompson Twins?

QUESTION 2
The duo James and Bobby Purify had their only two hit singles in 1976. Name both of them.

QUESTION 3
The 1994 single 'Do You Remember the First Time' was the Top 40 debut by which group?

QUESTION 4
Which 2006 Top 3 single by the Pussycat Dolls featuring will.i.am features a string sample from Electric Light Orchestra's 'Evil Woman'?

QUESTION 5
Who comes next in this sequence: Daz Sampson, Scooch, Andy Abraham, Jade Ewen... ?

QUESTION 6
Which of Level 42's Top 10 hits has the subtitle '(Living it Up)'?

QUESTION 7
Which member of the group Argent wrote Hot Chocolate's 'So You Win Again', 'Since You've Been Gone' by Rainbow, 'New York Groove' by Hello and 'No More the Fool' by Elkie Brooks?

QUESTION 8
Jimmy Somerville's 1989 debut solo hit featured June Miles-Kingston and was the cover of a late Sixties French song written by Serge Gainsbourg and recorded by Françoise Hardy. What is it called?

QUESTION 9
What is the surname of 'Dan' in the Seventies duo England Dan and John Ford Coley?

QUESTION 10
Perfect Symmetry, Hopes and Fears, Under the Iron Sea and Strangeland are Keane's four studio albums to date. All four reached number one, but in what order were they released?

Q1
Menudo

Q2
Brian Holland, Lamont Dozier, Eddie Holland

Q3
They all have one-word titles

Q4
'We Got the Whole World in Our Hands'

Q5
Paloma Faith (female coaches on each UK series of The Voice)

Q6
'Maybe that's What it Takes' (Top 3), 'Cry' (Top 20)

Q7
Franz Ferdinand, Sparks

Q8
'Rock 'N' Roll Mercenaries'

Q9
Silver Convention

Q10
'I Got the...'

answers

QUIZ 169
CHAMPIONS (9)

Q1
The Stylistics

Q2
'Misfit', 'Under the Thumb'

Q3
The Times they Are a-Changin'

Q4
Mark Moore

Q5
Shaved Fish

Q6
Terrorvision

Q7
'White Horses', 'Rupert'

Q8
1978

Q9
Tribute

Q10
Bill Haley & His Comets

BOOKS

THE ULTIMATE ROCK GUIDE

To answer the questions below and find out about 794 other locations worthy of pilgrimage in Britain and Ireland you'll need the second edition of Rock Atlas by David Roberts. It is packed with music facts including album cover locations, historic gigs, memorials, statues and much, much more!

Where can I shop in the world's oldest record store?

How do I find the Jimi Hendrix statue?

Where is the real Stawberry Field?

Which famous park has a musical bench in memory of Ian Dury?

Where is the spooky location for 1970's Black Sabbath album cover?

In which pub did Arctic Monkeys make their debut?

"**With Rock Atlas lying around it's impossible to resist leafing through to see which rock star lived, died, debauched or recorded near you**"

Mail on Sunday

On sale now

For information on Red Planet books, visit :www.redplanetzone.com

BOOKS

DEAD STRAIGHT GUIDES

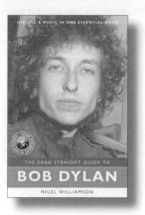

DEAD STRAIGHT GUIDES tell the complete story of a band or artist – giving you a guide to their lives and recordings that's informative and enjoyable to read. Written to appeal whatever your level of knowledge, they're accessible enough for the newcomer, but detailed enough for the diehard fan.

On sale now

For information on Red Planet books, visit :www.redplanetzone.com

Answers

QUIZ 170
CHAMPIONS (10)

Q1
Tom Bailey, Alannah Currie, Joe Leeway

Q2
'I'm Your Puppet', 'Morning Glory'

Q3
Pulp

Q4
'Beep'

Q5
Josh Dubovie (UK Eurovision Song Contest entries from 2006 to 2010)

Q6
'The Sun Goes Down'

Q7
Russ Ballard

Q8
'Comment te Dire Adieu'

Q9
Seals

Q10 Hopes and Fears ('04), Under the Iron Sea ('06), Perfect Symmetry ('08), Strangeland ('12)

175

About the authors

Neil Myners on **Phil Swern**

Paths cross in radio with alarming frequency. I've known Phil since the late Nineties, although it would be a few years before we began working together. He was producer of *Pick of the Pops* with Alan Freeman whilst I was working with 'Fluff' on his light classics show *Their Greatest Bits*; we'd regularly chat at the weekly BBC Radio 2 playlist meetings; we both freelanced at the same production company. Add to this a mutual love of record-collecting, albeit with vastly different sized libraries, meant working with 'Dr Pop' seemed a natural progression. That chance arose when Phil kindly asked if I'd like to work with him on ideas he had for Radio 2.

We quickly found the best business and programme plotting was done over lunch at La Vigna, an excellent though now-defunct Italian restaurant. Our first collaboration was a 2002 special celebrating the 50th anniversary of the charts. This was quickly followed by *Twos on 2* – a show about the greatest songs to reach number two. A simple but very effective idea from the mind of Mr Swern, it led to a compilation album and many more special programmes. All our co-productions were Phil's ideas. I was just very pleased to be asked along for the ride.

In the spring of 2003, Phil asked if I'd join the PopMaster team. This request felt a bit surreal as, along with countless other radio listeners at home, I'd enjoyed my daily dose of being an armchair contestant since it started. Twelve years later and here we are with book number two. I'm still very grateful to him for the opportunity to work on this much-loved quiz.

Phil Swern on **Neil Myners**

When Ken Bruce and his producer at the time, Colin Martin, invited me to help develop a quiz for their new-look Radio 2 show, we sat over an enjoyable lunch and a bottle or two of Merlot and devised PopMaster. It has now been running daily since 1996.

My job was to write all the questions, make up the music clips for the bonus rounds and deliver them a final package, which I continued to do for five years. But then I found it was taking up half my working week. So I decided to recruit a couple of colleagues – Shaun Greenfield to help with the questions and Simon Bray with the music clips. However, in 2003 Shaun realized he could no longer dedicate his time to the project, so I had the task of finding a new co-compiler.

My first thought was Neil Myners, as we had worked together on a number of various bank holiday specials for Radio 2. I was delighted when he agreed to take on the challenge and he has continued to work with me on the questions ever since.

When I suggested the idea of producing a PopMaster book to Red Planet, they were really enthusiastic about the concept and quickly commissioned it. I immediately invited Neil to co-write with me. This second volume was decided upon at quite short notice and it was only Neil who persuaded me that we could prepare it in time for the publication deadline. It's thanks to him that you are holding this edition of the PopMaster Quiz Book right now.